FAILING AMERICA

ROME DIDN'T CRUMBLE IN A

DAY EITHER

By: Richard Campagna

Cover design by Travis Retter

First Edition

View Rich's Blog at www.capitalfailure.net/blog

Email: Rich@capitalfailure.net

Follow Rich on Twitter: @richcamp21

Special thanks to my wife Sally who persevered with me through the frustrating times that inspired me to write this book and to my son Richard who took much time out of his busy work and family schedule to edit this book and make great suggestions on design and promoting this work.

PROLOGUE

Much has been written about the fall of the Roman Empire. Many empires have existed throughout history but none has had such a profound effect on our way of life. Much of our language is derived from Latin. Our architecture, engineering, law and forms of government are derived from what the Romans accomplished. Perhaps that is the source of our fascination with this empire. It is estimated that the Roman Empire ruled over 20% of the then known world. Today the U.S. comprises about 4% of the population of the world.

So why compare America to Rome? That was in an ancient world. It has no bearing on us, right? Rome was the economic, military and technological superpower of its time. Two thousand years ago they had well-developed written laws, a uniform currency, a system of weights and measures and even running water in their homes. Most Roman citizens lived their lives in their local civitas, a local unit of government something like the American county. Today, the U.S. is the clear superpower of the world in all of these categories. But we are declining quickly.

Many theories have been postulated as to what caused Rome to fall. The key factors most agree on are:

1. The deterioration of its economic condition:
   a. Many feel this deterioration was caused by the hoarding of bullion, the currency of the time. Without adequate currency the empire could not economically support its sprawling empire.
      i. Could this be happening in America today? The majority of the wealth in America is held by a very small percentage of the population and these people are using their economic power to ensure the concentration of wealth continues. No, they are not hoarding bullion but they are hoarding our currency in their own way.

2. The decline of its powerful army:
   a. At its peak the Roman army was so feared that no one dared attack them. The lack of enemies led to complacency and the army weakened and was susceptible to attack and the Roman Empire eventually was attacked on many fronts.
      i. Today our biggest war, the one that threatens America most does not involve armies with guns; it involves computers, test tubes and sophisticated manufacturing techniques. Our battle is

to remain the economic and technological superpower. Our success has lulled us into complacency and we now have the distinction of possessing an education system ranked near the bottom of developed countries in the world. Our position at the top is under siege and we are losing this battle.

3. The Senate became corrupt with many being easily bribed. Almost all of the power belonged to a distinct few:

   a. Prominent historian Ramsay MacMullen argues that a key factor in Rome's fall was the steady loss of focus and control over government as its aims were thwarted for private gain by high-ranking bureaucrats and military leaders.

      i. Our government today is legally bought and paid for. Wealthy individuals and large corporations use their money to elicit legislative favors that only they benefit from. Barely a day goes by without a news release of a politician somewhere being accused of accepting bribes or misusing funds. The majority of these favors are obtained through legal means.

It happened to Rome, the world's greatest superpower in A.D. 476. It can happen today to the world's greatest superpower. We as a people must understand what is driving the decline of our nation and demand change from our elected leaders. The unfortunate truth is that few understand what is happening to America. This book is intended to change that.

INTRODUCTION

Every four years about 125 million Americans (about 60% of those eligible to vote) go to the polls to elect the person who will lead our nation for the next four years. Most have little idea about the major issues of today; the poor decisions our government makes; the excessive spending and personal and corporate tax issues that are leading America to insolvency; and the excessive amounts the United States spends on education and health care, only to be ranked among the bottom of developed countries of the world in both categories.

This cannot be the right direction, America! We are no longer "one nation... indivisible" to which so many of us pledged allegiance every morning in school throughout our youth. Our Government is splintered into two parties who cannot work together and cannot compromise for the good of the nation. Each year Congress passes hundreds of meaningless laws but when it comes to solving the major issues threatening America, spending, insufficient tax revenue, immigration, health care and education, they are paralyzed by partisan politics. Our middle class, the people who built America are slowly disappearing, transforming us into a nation of "haves" and "have nots," not unlike many third world countries around the world. New immigrants continue to come to live in

America but not to be Americans.

Our government's financial position is trending into a position our children and grandchildren will suffer with for decades to come. We are not likely to become a third world country but for many of our citizens that is their reality. Our rights are being violated for the benefit of "special interests" - the super wealthy, big business, minorities, illegal immigrants and the poor and unmotivated. Our politicians are inept and destroying this country - it is time to take America back!

I sit here pondering what's happening to this great nation of ours, and I can't help but wonder what will be left for my grandchildren. We are no longer a nation whose new inhabitants exhibit allegiance to the country that gives them so much opportunity. Our entire government has become dysfunctional, the welfare and healthcare systems are fraught with abuse, and illegal immigrants are costing taxpayers billions of dollars. We spend almost twice as much per capita on health care as most developed countries in the world yet those countries manage to provide health care to everyone while in the U.S. tens of millions of our citizens have no health care. Our life expectancy in the U.S. is less than that of countries spending far less on health care. Our uninsured citizens and even many of those with insurance are one accident or illness away from total financial devastation. Many families with both parents working full time cannot afford health care. We spend more per capita on education than all but four countries in the developed world yet our education system ranks 25th in the world. Don't clean your glasses, you read that correctly. Are we really developing the leaders and inventors of tomorrow, leaders who will ensure that future generations of Americans enjoy the prosperity that so many of us have enjoyed?

The tax laws are being dictated by the minute minority who already hold the vast majority of the total wealth. The wealthiest Americans are garnering an ever increasing percentage of the total wealth, thanks to tax laws that allow the very richest to pay taxes at the lowest rates on a majority of their income. Yet it is not only the wealthy that are benefitting from the tax system. The very poor also benefit greatly by a system that rewards irresponsibility and makes it easy to obtain thousands of dollars in tax credits that many are not legally entitled to receive.

Financially, the government of America is a total failure. Our deficits and debt are overwhelming. There is no end in sight as the debt of the U.S. Government continues to grow to unimaginable levels. In late 2011, Washington was locked in a stalemate to resolve the country's debt ceiling. After a last minute compromise that narrowly avoided a default on the national debt, a major ratings agency took the unprecedented step of downgrading our nation's risk of default. This downgrade basically states that there is an increased likelihood that U.S. government bonds, historically viewed as the most risk-free of all investments, may not ultimately be paid back in the future! Unfortunately, the U.S. Government continues to borrow forty cents of every dollar it spends.

Remember when they used to call America the great melting pot? Today it's more of a mixing pot were many of the immigrant groups want to have their own mini nations within America. Unfortunately, our inept government seems to support this notion in the name of freedom. When millions of immigrants migrated to America from Europe their goal was to be Americans. To own businesses and support the great country that was America. Many of today's immigrants want to live in America but do not want to be Americans. They want to place their own holidays and customs ahead of those of America. Yet many are happy to collect the billions of dollars in government aid handed to them even though they may not even be citizens.

It's time Americans woke up to what is happening. This book will explain in brief, understandable terms the main issues that are destroying the greatest nation on earth, issues which too few Americans understand. Every great empire in the history of the world has fallen at some point – including Rome, the greatest empire in the history of the world. Do not think for a moment that "it can't happen to the USA." America is at a turning point – continuing on our current trajectory of political ineptitude and population-wide apathy and ignorance will doom "the land of the free and the home of the brave" to crumble just as every other major empire in the history of the world has crumbled.

So what factors are contributing most to America's downfall? Five things are leading our demise:

1. Inept Federal Government
2. An overly complex and unsustainable tax system
3. Our prohibitively expensive health care system
4. One of the world's most expensive yet poorest performing education systems
5. Big Business - Subjected to the highest corporate tax rates in the world yet the most profitable of them pay little or no tax.

I will address each separately in the chapters that follow. These are issues that every voting American should understand but does not have the time or the energy to research.

This is a brief lesson in taxes, economics and where our government spends our money for those that are not accountants, economists, or politicians. It also addresses the two areas where a major portion of government spending takes place, education and health care, yet these are areas where the U.S. is drastically underperforming most of the developed world. This book is simply seeking to give everyday working people an overview of what we are up against and to try to mobilize Americans to save our country before it's too late. Americans should know these things before they go to the polls. In the end I will offer some thoughts on how I would fix each of these given the ability to do so. Somebody better do something soon. I hope I have by offering this to you.

CHAPTER 1

FEDERAL GOVERNMENT

Part I, Economics

Should Our Government be Fired?

So, our government is totally inept. I think we all know that. Well, everyone except the people running our government. They have driven America to the brink of bankruptcy. But why should they worry? They did it by bowing to every special interest lobby imaginable in order to win votes and get reelected. They will have free top of the line health care for life, a generous pension and big fees for consulting when they retire. They get to vote their own pay increases and the terms under which their benefits and pensions can be changed. They ultimately decide who they can accept money from in order to keep their machine going. They are becoming millionaires because they are allowed to trade on insider information they receive as a result of their positions in Congress and on various committees. Some of these unfair advantages would land you or me in prison if we were to leverage them.

Think of the U.S. Government as being like a corporation. The President is the CEO, Congress is the Board of Directors, the Court system is the regulators and we, the people, are the shareholders. The only difference is that in the case of government the Board does not select the CEO, the shareholders do. If the Board doesn't like the way the CEO is running a private company they fire him and hire a new one. If the shareholders don't like what the board is doing they are free to elect a new board.

Our Insurmountable Debt

In corporate America if a company is borrowing funds to pay debts and its outflow exceeds the revenue it is taking in over an extended period of time, that company is considered insolvent. The deficit (annual budget shortfall) for the Federal government of the United States for 2010 was $1.4 trillion. That amounts to over $4,500 for every person in America. Since approximately 45% of all households in America pay no income tax, this amounts to approximately $8,200 for every person in a household that pays income tax. Sure some of that 45% is comprised of seniors with limited income but the fact remains only a little over half of all households actually pay income tax. Almost all of those who pay no income tax earn less than $40,000 per year.

The total debt of the United States is currently approximately $14,000,000,000,000 (that's $14 trillion), and it is growing by the minute. This equates to approximately $45,000 for every man, woman and child in America and $82,000 for each person in a taxpaying household. I equate this to taxpaying households simply because the Federal government has one source of income, taxes.

My first grandchild, Brooke, is the cutest little thing but apparently not very smart and totally irresponsible because at the tender age of eighteen months she has already accumulated $82,000 in debt. Unfortunately she lives in one of those taxpaying households. I think I need to talk to her about responsible spending. I will do that as soon as she learns to talk. How will she ever pay it back? At 5% interest she can start paying $357 per month immediately and it will be paid off by the time she hits 65 years old. I hope she gets a really good job soon because she obviously can't afford to waste time going to school.

America is borrowing money to pay its bills including paying the interest on its debt. In fact America borrows forty cents out of every dollar it spends. Try that at home. This is certainly the profile of a failed economic state.

Let's compare this to one of the greatest corporate failures in the history of the U.S. While comparisons of corporations to government are not an exact match, let's do it anyway, just for fun. In 2008 General Motors reported revenue of $148 billion. It also reported Debt of $45 billion and pension and postretirement benefit liabilities of $53 billion. This totals $98 billion of debt against $148 billion of revenue or debt equal to 66% of revenue. In 2009 General Motors filed for bankruptcy. The U.S. Government, on the other hand, currently has $14 trillion of debt. In 2008 the US Government collected tax revenue of $2.5 trillion. Of that, 42% was individual income tax, 36% from payroll tax (Social Security, Medicare, Unemployment...) and 12% was corporate income tax. So with $2.5 trillion of revenue and $14 trillion of debt the government's debt is 560% of revenue or about 8.5 times the level of GM's. Let's recall that at 66% GM declared bankruptcy. An over simplified example? Of course government is different. If it chooses to it can increase its revenue to almost any amount by increasing taxes. A corporation doesn't have that luxury. Their revenue is dependent on people they cannot force to buy their products. But does this comparison tell us anything about where are we heading?

So why not just decide not to pay more than we collect? Obviously government is more complex with the need to spread the wealth and help the poor and less fortunate. The mother on welfare gets the same vote as the billionaire. How do we satisfy everyone in a society where so many feel entitled to be provided for? Should we tell the poor, "too bad if you have nothing to eat, too bad if your baby is sick?" Of course not, but a line has to be drawn at some point. Even if the annual deficit were reduced to $1 trillion (an almost unrealistic 28% reduction), in ten years the federal debt will be $24 trillion. That would equate to $76,000 for every person in America and $140,000 for every person (including children) in a taxpaying household. In ten short years! Can you afford a second mortgage, because that is effectively what you will have if this continues?

In 2011, Congress and President Obama engaged in a months-long battle to come to a compromise to increase the amount of debt the US Government is allowed to incur in order to avoid a default on the national debt by the "wealthiest" country in the world. The U.S. was weeks from being unable to pay its bills. Of course, a last minute compromise was reached and this tragedy was averted, but we came perilously close to an event that would have generated worldwide economic shock of enormous proportions. Of course, our congressional leaders would be in a position to continue to feast on the now scarce filet mignon and red wine – only average Americans like you and I would be stuck to feast on saltines and tap water.

OK, so here is an obvious question for many, why doesn't the U.S. Government just print more dollars to pay debts and stimulate the economy? Why don't we just keep borrowing and printing U.S. dollars to pay it? Why not just print $1 trillion in $100 bills, pack it into about 200 tractor trailers, yes 200 tractor trailers, and take it to the local branch of Wells Fargo and ask to deposit it into a government account? Deficit solved for this year. The answer is devaluation and inflation. The more money we print the less it is worth against other currencies so the less we can afford to buy with our dollars in international markets. Remember, much of what we buy today is imported from other countries. This includes most of our oil, clothing, food and many other items. A devaluation of the dollar will result in a price increase. Printing dollars will cause massive inflation because more dollars will create more demand for goods. That drives up prices and now our more dollars are essentially worth no more than our fewer dollars were before – an unsustainable spiral that accomplishes little. As Nobel Prize-winning economist Milton Friedman put it, "the pieces of green paper have value because everybody thinks they have value." So with more currency floating around and the same economy behind them each dollar is worth less, hence devaluation.

Who Should Pay the Debt?

The Democrats want to increase taxes on the rich and the Republicans want to cut spending (programs). Now if it were totally up to the Democrats they would tax and spend us into oblivion - the deficit would continue to grow until it was beyond our ability to ever pay (it might already be). Why not? The people who won't work and keep having lots of babies deserve more and more federal assistance. Right? Then we will make them buy health insurance and if they can't afford it we will give them money to buy it. Give them $1,000 per child in the form of tax credits. Give them thousands of dollars in Earned Income Credits for having babies. So, let's tax the people who worked hard to get ahead and happened to make a lot of money as a result. Let's remember, 45% of all households in America pay no income tax at all and in fact many actually have a negative income tax.

What about those people who can't work – the sick and elderly? What about the person who grew up poor and mommy and daddy couldn't send them to Harvard? The ones who grew up working hard and continue to do so, sometimes working several jobs to try to make a better life for their children - should we as a society be willing to help them? In the Democrats' world, we would – we would just keep on spending and taxing.

Now the Republicans, especially the Tea Party, have the right idea. Cut Social Security and Medicare. Let the old people eat dog food. Let the poor kids get sick from infections in their gums because they couldn't afford to go to the dentist. The wealthy need a break too. If left to them, the budget reductions would be accomplished on the backs of our poorest and most vulnerable citizens while the rich would all be buying a second Ferrari. Think the rich are just getting richer? You bet. The richest 1% of the population takes home 24% of the income today as compared with 9% in 1976. According to the New York Times, from 1985 to 2005, 80% of the increase in wealth in America went to the richest 1%. We need to help them out. How is the guy making $1 million per year going to afford another $40,000 in income taxes if we repeal the Bush Tax Cuts on those earning over $250,000? Is there no compassion? Don't the rest of us understand how much it costs to fill the gas tank on a forty foot yacht? Do you have any idea how much it costs to fly a family of four first class to Hawaii and stay seven nights in the Ritz Carlton? These people need a break too, you know.

In 2009, the total net worth of the 400 richest Americans (according to Forbes) was $1.27 trillion. In 2009 the bottom 60% of U.S. households, representing about 180 million Americans, owned only 2.3% of total U.S. wealth, or $1.22 trillion. In other words, the 400 richest Americans are worth MORE than the 180 million "poorest" Americans! Sure, some achieved success because they worked harder, some because they were smarter or had a great business idea and some because of a head start in life, although no one seems ready to admit that. What else helped them? A tax and financial system designed to help the rich get richer.

Need any more evidence that the rich have money to throw away but can't possibly afford any more taxes? In August, 2011, the New York Times published an article that stated Nordstrom has a waiting list for a Chanel sequined tweed coat with a $9,010 price and that Neiman Marcus has sold out in almost every size of Christian Louboutin "Bianca" platform pumps, at $775 a pair. If you can afford a $9,000 coat and $800 shoes will it really hurt to pay a little more in taxes?

So who is right – the Democrats or the Republicans? The answer is that both are right and both are wrong. When will our leaders realize that this is a two pronged issue: excessive spending and inadequate revenue? We cannot even begin to reasonably slow down the progression of our demise without addressing both.

Let's do some math just for fun. 54% of the government's revenue comes from income taxes (42% individual and 12% corporate). The actual deficit for 2010 is $1.4 trillion and forecasted to be $1.6 trillion for 2011. Let's assume the incredibly competent members of Congress and the President can, by some miracle, work out a compromise and reduce the deficit. Assume a $1 trillion annual deficit (probably an excessively optimistic assumption), arbitrarily reduced from the current amount. Anyway, at $1 trillion of deficit, individual and corporate income taxes would have to be increased 74% just to eliminate the deficit. This is on top of assumed cuts in spending to reduce the deficit by 29% to get it down to $1 trillion. Everyone in favor, please raise your hands. One thing is clear, however - taxes are too low in this country (some specific analysis on that in Chapter II).

Here's a brain teaser for you: Members of congress are elected by a straight popular vote. You need 51% to win an election. They are supposed to represent the constituents of the area from which they are elected. Only 1.5% of the population earns over $250,000 and let's assume that each of those $250,000+ earners votes for a particular candidate.

That means that 97% of the people who voted for that person earn less than $250,000. So why are Republicans fighting so hard to reduce taxes for the people who represent such a small fraction of the votes they received? Could it be that these voters represented a much higher percentage of their campaign contributions? Is it a surprise that Mitt Romney, republican candidate for President disclosed that his tax rate is about 15% because most of his income is from capital gains? In 2012 Republicans are not only fighting tooth and nail to keep the capital gains tax at 15%, well below what many of us pay on much smaller incomes, but some of them have proposed to eliminate this tax all together!

Where Does Our Money Go?

What would need to happen to balance the budget through cuts in spending? Here are some facts to consider. The Congressional Budget Office estimates total spending for 2011 at $3.7 trillion. Keep in mind the estimated total tax revenue of the U.S. Government for 2011 is estimated at $2.2 trillion. The spending breaks down as follows:

Table 1

Mandatory Spending - $2.1 Trillion		
• 34% Social Security Payments	$714 billion
• 38% Medicare and Medicaid	$735 billion
• 20% Income Security & Retirement Benefits – Unemployment, Food Stamps, Housing Assistance, Disability, Federal Pensions	$420 billion
Discretionary Spending – $1.6 Trillion		
• 54% Defense	$864 billion
• 43% Domestic Programs - Agricultural Subsidies, Environment, Education, Transportation,	$688 billion
• 3% - International	$48 billion
Interest Payments - $.2 Trillion		$200 billion

Mandatory spending programs are generally determined by eligibility rules, formulas, and other parameters set by Congress in legislation. Mandatory spending does not have to be approved by Congress: it happens automatically even if Congress doesn't vote for it and can only be changed by new legislation. Think of it as a commitment the government has made like you paying your mortgage every month. Discretionary spending is spending that Congress has to vote for generally as part of the annual budget process. It does not get funded automatically. This might be that part of your spending that you allocate for entertainment.

This table shows the quandary the government currently has to deal with. In effect, total revenue is just enough to cover mandatory spending; while the government borrows all of the rest. Discretionary spending as a percentage of the total budget has already been reduced in the past forty years. Mandatory spending has become a much larger share of the federal budget over the past four decades, more than doubling from about 25% of federal spending in 1962 to just over half today. The share of the budget going for discretionary spending has fallen from 66% in 1962 to about 40% now.

Let's look at what your household would look like if you ran it like the U.S. Government.

	Household	Government
Total Income	$ 75,000	$ 2,200,000,000,000
Total Spending	$ 126,136	$ 3,700,000,000,000
Borrowed Money	$ 51,136	$ 1,500,000,000,000
Total Loans	$ 477,273	$ 14,000,000,000,000

Could you imagine ever running your household like that?

So where do we cut to balance the budget? There are many misconceptions as to where the government spends its money. Some think we can balance the budget by cutting spending on government. The actual costs of running the government are a small part of total spending as are the amounts we spend on things like international aid.

Cutting Social Security is tantamount to breaking a direct promise mainly to our elderly citizens. For decades they had money withheld from their pay specifically to fund Social Security. It was put in a separate fund in order to provide for their retirement. Income taxes were supposed to cover the other expenditures. Now that government has been totally mismanaged some in Congress want to reduce Social Security benefits. Many of our elderly citizens barely survive on their meager benefits – a cut would be catastrophic for them. In all fairness to our government leaders, they didn't cause the Social Security deficits that are on the horizon. A root cause of the Social Security funding problem is the fact that people are simply living longer than previously anticipated and therefore collecting benefits for a longer period of time.

Payroll taxes, mainly Social Security and Medicare taxes will total $818 billion in 2011, well below the level of expenditures. Social security has actually been covering its own expenditures through payroll taxes and interest earnings on its trust fund although in 2010 it ran a paltry $46 billion deficit due to reduced payroll taxes caused by increased unemployment. That deficit came out of the Social Security Trust Fund. Today it is essentially adding zero to the deficit. The future is not so clear. As more people retire that will change and it will run a deficit and the fund is expected to be exhausted by 2037, though that estimate changes with each new analysis. Two answers exist to save Social Security. Well, two answers other than screwing our senior citizens out of the money they put into social security for fifty years.

1. Reduce benefits either directly or by increasing the retirement age. Some have proposed raising the retirement age to 70 years of age. The difficult part

here is that for people involved in physically strenuous occupations, working to 70 may not be an option.

2. Increase the tax rate or the wage base upon which we pay Social Security Taxes. In 2011 we only paid Social Security taxes of 4.2% (normally 6.2% but Congress lowered it for only 2011 as an economic stimulus) and our employer pays an additional 6.2% on the first $106,800 of wages. If you make more than that you do not pay Social Security taxes on the amount over $106,800. For many low to mid wage earners, Social Security taxes are more than their income taxes. Also consider that Social Security taxes are only paid on earned salary and self employment income, not on investment, including capital gains, or other income. The marginal impact at different earnings levels is as follows:

Table 2

Earned Income	Social Security Tax	Percent of Earnings
$106,800	$6,622	6.2%
$250,000	$6,622	2.6%
1,000,000	$6,622	.7%

In fairness to our millionaire friends, Social Security benefits paid upon retirement are only based on the maximum taxable earnings so everyone in this example would pay the same total tax and receive the same monthly benefit when they reach retirement age.

Medicare on the other hand is a different story. We can see in the table on page 25 that Medicare and Medicaid pays out more per year than Social Security. The problem is that Social Security collects a tax equal to 12.4% of payroll while Medicare collects a tax of 2.9% of payroll. The Medicare trust fund is projected to run out of money by 2024. The distinction between Medicare and Medicaid – Medicare is funded by the Medicare tax and provides medical care to citizens 65 years of age and older. Medicaid, generally run by the states provides medical care for people who cannot afford to pay. For 2012 the Federal Government is budgeted to pay $270 billion in grants to states for Medicaid.

What is causing these shortfalls?

- Inadequate tax revenue to fund benefit levels caused by rates being too low and payroll being lower than expected. There are many baby boomers retiring and an inadequate number of people paying in.
- Higher quality healthcare – healthcare advancements are resulting in people living longer and longer and

therefore collecting benefits under these programs for a longer period of time. In addition, this enhanced health care is very expensive and much of that cost is borne by Medicare. More and more life saving care is available but at a very high cost.

How can Medicare be saved:

1. Increase payroll tax amounts. There is likely no way for Medicare to remain solvent without an increase. Some forecasts show costs declining, though we have seen over and over again that these rosy predictions don't come true.

2. Reduce costs of Medicare.

    a. Today doctors run many unnecessary tests out of fear of lawsuits. These tests, MRI's, CT Scans etc, are very costly. Tort (lawsuit) reform could go a long way toward helping but the American Bar Association, representing lawyers who benefit greatly from these lawsuits, is very powerful (or put another way, has a lot of money to give to legislators.)

    b. Reengineer the system. We must revise the system of billing that results in gross overstatement of costs, especially when Medicare or health insurance is involved. One brief personal example just for fun: I recently had a bulging disk in my back so painful I couldn't even stand up. It was excruciating. I went to an urgent care center figuring it would be a lot cheaper than an emergency room visit. I was in there for twenty minutes. The doctor listened, then gave me a shot of pain killer and wrote a prescription for a pain killer and a muscle relaxer. A few weeks later I got a bill for $449. My new insurance was not yet effective so when the insurance declined it they sent me a revised bill for $339. I was in shock. I called the billing department and said it was outrageous. I explained I had no insurance. The nice lady on the phone said the charge was based on guidelines of allowable charges but since I was uninsured and self paying, the bill would only be $70. I guess if I had been on Medicare they would have paid $449 or $349 or certainly a lot more than $70.

c. Put more resources into investigating billing as we hear almost weekly about big, fraudulent Medicare schemes.

Certainly there is more to it than this but the short answer is that revenue is nowhere close to the amount needed to keep this program alive.

An in depth look at where all government spending goes is beyond the scope of this book but available online. In the appendix to this book I have included a more detailed summary of the White House Budget showing where the U.S. Government spends its money.

What are our other alternatives? Do we want to cut food stamps to the poor? Unemployment benefits to the millions of Americans who have already lost their homes and are now living on relatives' couches or in shelters with their children? How about eliminating airports or the security at them - we can just take our chances with terrorists. Should we reduce defense spending in this time of worldwide conflicts?

In reality, we need to do both, cut spending and raise taxes. Unfortunately, those with the ability to absorb more taxes are the rich and middle class. Let's remember that under our current structure the rich continue to get disproportionately richer. Once again, 80% of the growth in wealth over the past 20 years has gone to the top 1%. Is this what America was built on? No. It was built on a strong middle class that is finding it harder and harder to support their families.

We are hearing proposals from Congress related to the debt crisis to cut $3 trillion or $4 trillion over the next ten years. Based on our current trajectory, our deficit before those cuts over the next ten years would be another $10 to $14 trillion. These proposals will only make a small dent in the growth of our national debt, let alone stop the growth of debt completely.

Some really hard decisions have to be made and a tax increase is one of them. There is no way America can get back on sound financial footing without a lot of pain on both the revenue and expenditure side. Even with such changes, it will likely take years of discipline to right the ship. Otherwise we will leave our children with a disaster.

The Congressional Budget Office has prepared projections of the Federal deficit. They are incredibly optimistic, in my opinion. You should know that these projections assume the following in the next five years:

- By 2016 personal income taxes are double the 2011 level[1]
- By 2016 corporate income taxes are double the 2011 level[1]
- Total spending, mandatory and discretionary increase by only 27%.
    1. Not the tax rate but the amount of taxes collected which essentially means economic activity doubles.

Let's also consider the realistic growth in debt assuming an annual deficit based on current deficit spending as there is currently no evidence that will change. A third scenario projects U.S. Debt assuming current deficits and a $2.5 trillion cut in spending that Congress has agreed to as part of the bill to raise the debt ceiling (although they have not yet determined how they will achieve those cuts). Do any of us have the confidence that these cuts will actually happen?

With these three scenarios the total debt of the U.S. Government looks like this:

Year	U.S Debt (CBO)	U.S Debt - Realistic	US Debt- With Proposed Cuts
2011	14.0	14.0	14.0
2012	15.1	15.4	15.2
2013	15.8	16.8	16.3
2014	16.3	18.2	17.5
2015	16.8	19.6	18.6
2016	17.4	21.0	19.8
2017	18.0	22.4	20.9
2018	18.6	23.8	22.1
2019	19.3	25.2	23.2
2020	20.0	26.6	24.4
2021	**20.7**	**28.0**	**25.5**

When will we stop this insane financial policy? Unless we drastically change the fiscal policies of the U.S. Government our debt will continue to progress upward. We are already beyond our ability to pay. This excessive spending cannot be solved through tax increases. The waste in our government spending is crippling America. But in the face of increased spending we continue to reduce taxes. The two causes of our deficits are moving in opposite directions exacerbating the situation.

What do they Mean – Bush Tax Cuts?

The top tax rates in this country have dropped precipitously in the past thirty years. In 1981 for a couple filing a joint return the top tax bracket was 70% on all earnings over $180,000. In today's dollars based on inflation increases that $180,000 would equate to about $432,000. The tax rate today on earnings over $380,000 is 35%. America's income tax as a percent of Gross Domestic Product and its maximum tax rates are near the lowest in the world (more specifics on that in Chapter II).

We all hear Congress and the President discussing repealing the Bush tax cuts on the wealthy, those earning over $250,000. What would that mean? The Bush cuts slightly changed the point at which certain tax brackets kicked in but basically they were a reduction in the top brackets. In addition the point at which the brackets are hit is inflated each year and so it changes automatically. To simplify, the main changes were as follows:

2002 Before Bush Tax Cuts Married Filing Jointly				2010 After Bush Tax Cuts Married Filing Jointly		
Marginal Tax Rate	Tax Brackets Over	But Not Over		Marginal Tax Rate	Tax Brackets Over	But Not Over
10.0%	$0	$12,000		10.0%	$0	$16,750
15.0%	$12,000	$46,700		15.0%	$16,750	$68,000
27.0%	$46,700	$112,850		25.0%	$68,000	$137,300
30.0%	$112,850	$171,950		28.0%	$137,300	$209,250
35.0%	**$171,950**	**$307,050**		**33.0%**	**$209,250**	**$373,650**
38.6%	**$307,050**	-		**35.0%**	**$373,650**	-

These do not represent big changes but a few percentage points in the higher tax brackets. However, they can be big if your earnings are in the millions of dollars. Big in dollars but not a significant amount in terms of the lifestyle lived by these people. In fact, if you are earning over $250,000 they probably don't impact your life at all. There is however another major change in the tax code that most certainly provides a big benefit to the top earners. Capital gains tax, the tax paid on the gain on sale of investments held for one year or longer was reduced from 25% to 15%. Who has the ability to hold significant investments and generate these tax advantaged gains? Is it likely the truck driver or school teacher down the street is generating substantial capital gains on their investment portfolios? Can it be that Republicans feel so strongly about a 3.6% change in the tax bracket that affects only about 1.5% of their constituents?

There are so many tax provision that impact individuals and corporations that trying to discuss them here would cause you to close this book and go to sleep. Our tax code is mind boggling, all because of provisions added to appease special interests, many of whom surely gave campaign contributions to members of Congress. The tax laws passed by Congress total about 3,400 pages and there is another approximately 14,000 pages of regulations issued by the IRS to explain and clarify the nonsense issued by Congress. The morass of special provisions, many benefitting only a single type of enterprise or situation, are mind boggling even to the greatest tax experts. We will look at some more detailed comparisons in Chapter II with a more in depth look at the tax structure and some of its issues.

Drastic change is needed to correct the economic crisis building in America. Today every taxpaying citizen, man, woman and child is carrying $82,000 of government debt and within ten years that amount will double to $160,000. Mandatory spending programs have grown to over $2 trillion annually and these programs alone equal the total tax revenue of the U.S. Government. Drastic cuts in Social Security, Medicare, Unemployment and other social programs would put our most vulnerable citizens at catastrophic risk. Yet as more and more of our citizens fall into financial hardship, the richest Americans continue to accumulate a larger share of the growth in wealth due to tax policies favorable to the wealthy. The rich get richer and those in the middle are vanishing.

Part II, Stupid Government

In any private enterprise the CEO and the Board of the USA would all have been fired years ago, but the American voting public keeps putting the same people in place. Why? Because there is no other choice. There is no independent thinking in Congress, only a bunch of drones doing exactly what the party leadership says.

Can it be any more obvious than in the passing of the health care legislation? Of 175 Republicans in the House of Representatives and 41 in the Senate, not a single one voted for health care reform. Is it possible that none of them thought health care reform was a good idea? Really?!?! Is there not one independent thinker in that entire group? The Republicans disagree with everything the Democrats do and vice versa - the two party system has outlived its useful life. We need a Congress where people are elected based on their views and they then vote based on those views. Perhaps I don't know the inner workings of Congress. Politicians would tell you that would never work. I am going to choose to disagree. Let the independent thinkers elect the leadership. Forget voting according to party. Vote based on what your constituents want. They elected you. They pay you.

The point is not whether health care reform was well conceived but come on, zero votes? In deference to the Republicans, this is a bad law. The liberal members of our government feel it is appropriate to put the burden of health care on the shoulders of private industry. The costs involved are astounding, thanks in part to our ill conceived health care system and private industry should not be asked to shoulder public needs that the government cannot. No other country asks private industry to shoulder the burden of health care for its citizens. The countries with the best health care systems surprisingly have public health care. More on that topic in Chapter III. This is not to praise the Democrats who are equally inept. Health care reform will certainly turn into one more form of welfare for the bottom dwellers of our society who have no interest in becoming productive members of society. They already get Social Security, Welfare, food stamps, unemployment, WIC, subsidized housing and about $40 billion per year in earned income credit on their taxes, a portion of which they are stealing (we will talk about that under income taxes). Now we will give them money so they can buy government mandated healthcare. It's the practices of the moronic health insurance companies and health care providers that need to be reformed...but more on that later too.

On another topic, why, after fifty years, can our Federal Government still not come to any conclusions on how to handle illegal immigration? There are, depending on the date and time you read the numbers, about 11 million illegal immigrants in the US. That's about 3.5% of our total population. These illegal immigrants represent 27% of prisoners in our jails. That makes them almost eight times as likely to end up in jail as the rest of us. These prisoners cost us, the taxpayers, billions per year to house, cloth, and feed. Still, doing something to control or curtail illegal immigration would result in lost votes for our friends in D.C. so we let it go. Don't want to piss off the mothers of the gang members or they might not vote for you.

Let's look at another example of how our Government is flushing our money down the drain. According to an ABC News Report, in 2005 Congress passed the Presidential $1 Coin Act ordering the US Mint to produce $1 coins to honor every dead president. The bill was introduced on May 17, 2005, by the moronic Senator John E. Sununu of New Hampshire with over 70 equally idiotic co-sponsors. Of course it took a majority of all the members of the House and Senate to pass it and President George Bush to sign it. What could they have been thinking? Today, and every day, the mint produces 2 million of these $1 coins. The problem is that nobody wants them, so they are produced and immediately sent to storage, at an additional storage cost of hundreds of thousands of dollars. Now the mint will spend $650,000 to build a new vault in Dallas Texas to store the unwanted coins. It will cost $3 million just to ship them to the new vault. Unless Congress passes a law to stop production they will continue to be produced for five more years. Billions of taxpayer dollars to produce coins no one wants only to ship them like radioactive waste to a vault for perpetual storage. They will most certainly never be used. Estimates are that the total cost will be $2 billion. Is that a lot? Not to our government. The US Government spends that amount about every 18 hours, assuming a $1 trillion annual deficit.

Let's put that cost in perspective. Most people can't even comprehend how much a billion dollars is. It is staggering how quickly billions add up. One billion minutes ago Jesus Christ was being crucified. If an average American Family of four needs $40,000 per year to have a decent life the $2 billion of waste that this program produced could have funded 50,000 families for a full year. Or put another way, if the government paid off $2 billion of debt with that money that is costing 5% interest they would save $100 million per year for the American taxpayer.

Finally, in July 2011, Congressman Jared Polis (D-CO) introduced the Cutting Out Inefficient and Needless Spending (COINS) Act, which would reform the wasteful Presidential $1 Coin program. The program is downsizing but not ended altogether. I say we melt the silver down and sell it while prices are high and return the money to America!

Our government's ineptitude is not limited to financial issues. They are also more interested in protecting the rights of illegals and criminals then law abiding, taxpaying American citizens.

How about the complete ineptitude at the Justice Department headed up by Eric Holder the US Attorney General? Consider the case of Sukhjinder Basra – who is incarcerated at the California Men's Colony in San Luis Obispo for a drug offense. The prison required him to trim his beard to within one-half inch in accordance with prison regulations. He refused under religious terms and was punished. So the Department of Justice is spending your tax dollars to sue the State of California to enforce this convicted drug dealer's right to an exemption from the rules that every other inmate has to follow.

"The rights guaranteed by the Constitution extend to all people in the United States," said Andre Birotte Jr., the U.S. Attorney for the Central District of California, in a press release. "By protecting those rights -- even for those incarcerated -- we strengthen those rights for all."

By requiring Basra to cut his beard, the state is compelling him to violate his religious beliefs in contravention of the Religious Land Use and Institutionalized Persons Act, the federal government alleges. "The freedom to practice one's faith in peace is among our most cherished rights," said Thomas E. Perez, assistant attorney general for the department's civil rights division.

Wow! Really? Do these imbeciles really believe that? Do you? Does anyone reading this really believe that this criminal's rights are being violated because he is required to abide by the same prison rules as every other prisoner? We all realize the job of the Justice Department is to uphold the laws of the United States, not to make them but how about a little test of the reasonably prudent man? Do you find it as amazing as I do that such a law even exists? Thank you President Clinton for signing this one. Stupid me, I thought prison was punishment for committing crimes and for which certain freedoms were supposed to be lost. I wonder how much each taxpayer in America and California will spend on this one.

Where was the Justice Department in Morgan Hill, California in May 2010? Administrators at Live Oak High School in Morgan Hill, California sent five students home after they refused to remove their American flag T-shirts and bandanas -- garments the school officials deemed "incendiary" on Cinco de Mayo.

The five teens were sitting at a table outside the school on Wednesday morning when Assistant Principal Miguel Rodriguez asked two of them to remove their American flag bandanas. The boys complied, but were asked to accompany Rodriguez to the principal's office.

The five students were then told they must turn their American Flag T-shirts inside-out or be sent home, though it would not be considered a suspension. Rodriguez told the students he did not want any fights to break out between Mexican-American students celebrating their heritage and those wearing American flags. More than 100 students were spotted wearing the colors of the Mexican flag -- red, white and green -- as they left school, including some who had the flag painted on their faces or arms, the Morgan Hill Times reported. Lis Wiehl, a former federal prosecutor and a Fox News legal analyst, said the incident appears to be a "blatant" violation of the students' First Amendment right to free speech.

America has become a concoction of independent nations who want to have their own little micro cultures that are superior to the ideals upon which America was built into the greatest nation on earth. I don't care what country you came from, you come here understanding that you are living as an American in the US where wearing the American Flag is an honor. Any person, who thinks otherwise, should go back to the country they came from. So, convicted drug felons are entitled to protection by the US Justice Department but to hell with the American citizens who want to proudly display the American flag? Are we really going to vote these people back into office? Is this what you want from your government?

Why is government dysfunctional? Because the people who run it are indebted to those who helped put them there. Who helped put them there? People and businesses with money. Oh yes, and the special voting groups who vote for the candidate who protects their own, illegal or not. These minorities are in many ways more prejudice than the whites they so criticize for being bigots. Let's look at one example:

When Sonia Sotomayor was nominated for the Supreme Court Senator John McCain opposed her because he did not agree she was objective. Comedian George Lopez came out and asked all Hispanics to vote McCain out of office. Why? Because he did not support the Hispanic nominee. Let's think about this - if Sotomayor was Italian or German and McCain objected to her do you think Italians or Germans would jump up and say "vote McCain out of office?" No, of course not. Lopez made his remarks based solely on her national origin, nothing else. This is the epitome of prejudice and an influential member of our society asking members of his minority group to vote a candidate out of office over issues of national origin. I respect McCain for standing up for what he thought was right and not giving in to special interests. We need more of that in our government.

Why do politicians want to be there? Prestige. Power. Attractive salaries. Excellent benefits - top of the line health care, generous pensions and when they leave, lucrative jobs with companies and industries they supported while in government. What if they were not allowed to go to work in industries they regulated or served on committees that regulated those industries? Congress passed the Sarbanes-Oxley ("SOX") act in response to the Enron and MCI frauds. This is a somewhat worthless piece of legislation that is costing American businesses billions simply to comply with paperwork requirements.

It requires public corporations to expend massive amounts of energy and cost to produce mountains of paperwork to document internal control processes and requires senior officers to sign attestations on the adequacy of those control processes. It also includes many provisions regarding auditors and their responsibilities.

It would have done nothing to stop the Enron or MCI frauds. Just like illegal firearms, the criminals will still have them. If you are a corporate executive intent on knowingly committing a massive fraud just to boost your share price and personal net worth is it likely that signing something acknowledging that you could suffer personal consequences for doing so will stop you?

I used to work for a large public accounting firm. Most people who didn't stay in public accounting, like me, took jobs with our clients. What better fit? We were top of the line finance and accounting professionals and already knew the company we audited. SOX said auditors could no longer go to work for their clients. They felt auditors would turn a blind eye to fraudulent accounting practices if they knew they would get a big job with the company after the audit was done. You scratch my back I'll scratch yours. Sounds a little like working in Congress. However, members of Congress are allowed to accept lucrative jobs with the companies and industries they regulated while in Congress. Doesn't that sound a bit like a double standard?

Now, if we said only the cream of the crop make it into elected positions we would all certainly have to say they deserve high pay and benefits as they would receive if they stayed in private industry. Unfortunately, based on their job performance currently, I doubt they would have made it in corporate leadership positions. They get elected based on their ability to obtain financial support from the wealthy and big business and excite the voting public, generally with promises we all should know they have no intention nor the ability to keep.

We are in the unique position in America where every citizen, regardless of race, religion, education, intelligence or income has one vote. So we can all vote for the candidate who represents our interest and not that of the money sources. Why don't we? Because those people can't run. It takes money, and a lot of it, to run for public office. Those people are too busy finding a way to eke out a living and put food on the table.

Many thought we had elected such a candidate in 2008 when support from "average Americans" elected Barack Obama President. He promised a new era. "Change we can believe in." What a lie. He is every bit the same as all other politicians.

During his campaign, Obama promised to diminish the clout of special interests and make the White House more accessible to everyday Americans. He blasted "the cynics, the lobbyists, the special interests," who he said had "turned our government into a game only they can afford to play." But the bundlers prevailed. A bundler is a person who sponsored or held some sort of fundraising effort on behalf of that candidate and raised a significant sum of money. They are not necessarily wealthy but know enough affluent people to raise money from them.

An iWatch News investigation found:

- Overall, 184 of 556, or about one-third, of Obama bundlers or their spouses joined the administration in some role. But the percentages are much higher for the big-dollar bundlers. Nearly 80 percent of those who collected more than $500,000 for Obama took "key administration posts," as defined by the White House. More than half of the ambassador nominees who were bundlers raised more than half a million.

- The big bundlers had broad access to the White House for meetings with top administration officials and glitzy social events. In all, campaign bundlers and their family members account for more than 3,000 White House meetings and visits. Half of them raised $200,000 or more.

So why doesn't the average Joe raise money and run for national office? Well, Joe can't raise the money to do so. He doesn't have the connections. Rich successful people have the contacts with rich successful people who contribute to campaigns. But let's be honest, is anyone going to vote for the maintenance worker with a high school education for Senator or worse yet, President. Of course not; or at least I hope not. But there are many bright, educated people who would be effective in Congress if they could get the chance. So government is not of the people, by the people or for the people. It is of, by and for those who can and do contribute money.

What do these few minor examples mean? Nothing by themselves. They are just a few examples among thousands of examples of the foolishness and incompetence of our government. Somehow, they must be held accountable for their actions and we need to have the information necessary to decide whether we want to vote them back into office. The unfortunate thing is that the American public has neither the knowledge of what is happening nor the time to research it in order to be well informed voters. Furthermore, because of the way in which people get elected there is little choice for the average American to vote for candidates who will truly look out for their best interests.

CHAPTER II

TAX SYSTEM

Part I - Overview

Every one of us, rich, middle class, or poor, thinks we pay too much in income taxes. The poor and the middle class think the rich pay too little and the rich think they pay too much. The poor, who not only don't pay taxes but get free handouts, think they get too little. The fact of the matter is that we do pay too little in taxes for the level of spending we want/need to maintain in this country – as a percentage of GDP, we are one of the lowest taxed nations in the world. The government of the United States needs a lot more revenue, pure and simple. Fixing it will require some pain on the part of all of us. There simply are not enough millionaires to cover the increase in revenue we need so increasing taxes only for the rich is not the answer. Let's look at some overall facts.

The Organisation for Economic Co-operation and Development (OECD) is an organization of developed countries around the world and works to promote policies that will improve the economic and social well-being of people around the world.   They perform numerous independent studies mainly on their member countries that are the leading developed countries in the world. You will see this organization referenced repeatedly throughout this book.

One way to measure taxes in relation to the economic size of a country is to measure taxes as a percentage of Gross Domestic Product ("GDP"). GDP refers to the market value of all completed goods and services produced within a country in a given period. Essentially it is a measure of the size of our economy. Of all the countries in OECD, only Mexico, Chile and Turkey have a lower tax as a percentage of GDP than the US. The US tax is about 25% lower than the average of all OECD member countries. The following chart produced by the OECD shows the details.

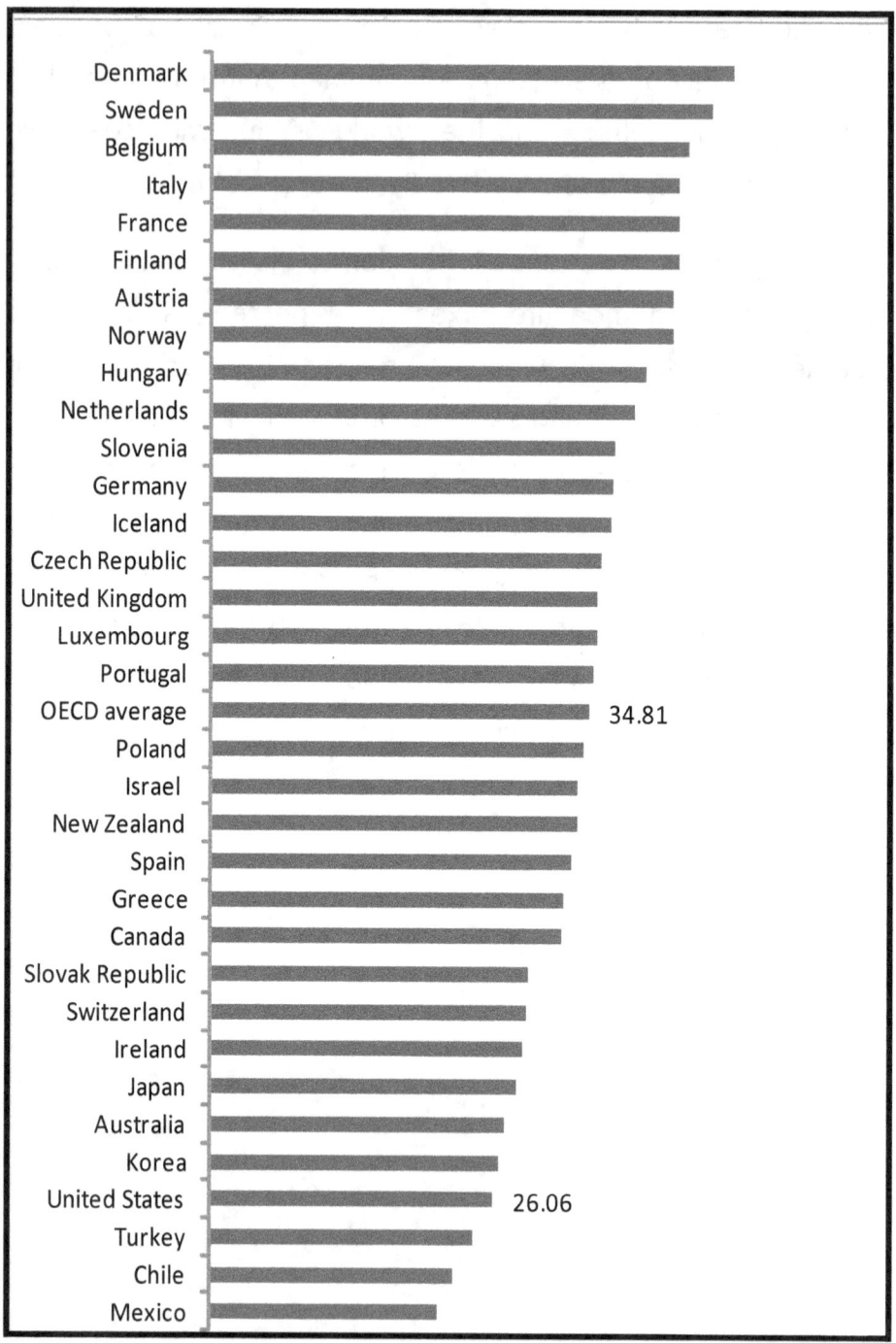

Denmark	
Sweden	
Belgium	
Italy	
France	
Finland	
Austria	
Norway	
Hungary	
Netherlands	
Slovenia	
Germany	
Iceland	
Czech Republic	
United Kingdom	
Luxembourg	
Portugal	
OECD average	34.81
Poland	
Israel	
New Zealand	
Spain	
Greece	
Canada	
Slovak Republic	
Switzerland	
Ireland	
Japan	
Australia	
Korea	
United States	26.06
Turkey	
Chile	
Mexico	

There is little question that the tax structure in America is helping the rich to get richer and the middle class to disappear. This is a capitalist country and there is nothing wrong with people getting rich by developing new ideas and launching new companies. After all, the rich are the people who employ everyone else - we need them. However, at a certain point of income and wealth, it all becomes excess well above the basic needs of food, clothing, and shelter. But wait, shouldn't the person who invented a new product and started a successful company live in a big house and drive a Bentley? Isn't this the American dream and the goal of Capitalism? Isn't this what made America the richest and greatest country in the world? Sure. God bless them. But our tax structure, and that of most developed countries was designed to take a bigger piece of that excess. The problem is that it really doesn't anymore. The percentage of income and net worth going to the top earners is growing unequally.

In the destruction of wealth that resulted from the Great Recession of 2007 to 2009, average declines in wealth were 16% for the richest fifth of Americans and 25% for the remaining four-fifths. The distribution of the wealth, even as the total amount shrank, was made more uneven due to larger drops in wealth for those at the bottom. The share of wealth held by the richest fifth of American households increased by 2.2 percentage points to 87.2%, while the remaining four-fifths gave up those 2.2 percentage points and held onto just 12.8% of all wealth. That bears repeating, 87% of the wealth is held by 20% of the households.

The published income tax rates are somewhat meaningless. After deduction for capital gains taxed separately at only 15%, deductions and credits for itemized deductions, standard deduction, personal exemptions, child tax credits, education/tuition credits, student loan interest credits, earned income credits, child care credits, retirement savings credits, foreign tax credits...you get the picture...the average tax rate paid by all taxpayers in 2008, the latest year for which the IRS has published data is only 12.2% of income. The top 1%, those earning over $380,354 paid 23.3% income tax. As discussed earlier, Social Security taxes make up a higher percent of income up to $106,800 in income, the point at which there is no more Social Security tax on wages. These numbers also exclude state income taxes which vary widely by state.

US Tax Revenues were $2.1 trillion in 2011. This includes personal and corporate income taxes as well as payroll taxes. If they were to increase to the OECD average of 34.8% that would represent over $500 billion in additional revenue, something that would go a long way toward resolving the deficit. Of course it isn't really that simple because raising taxes could result in a decrease in economic activity and higher unemployment which would increase required spending for things like unemployment and a decrease in revenue from income and payroll taxes. Perhaps now is not the time, given our economic situation, however, longer term tax increases must figure into the solution. Cutting spending alone will not begin to adequately reduce our deficits and to slow the growth in total debt.

Part II

Personal Income Taxes

We all know the rich earn a large portion of the income in America. In fact, the top 1% earned 24% of total earnings. Do they deserve it? Some do some don't. We constantly read about CEO's who rake in millions as their companies are floundering, only to be fired and given many more millions in severance. That's just the sheer stupidity of the Boards of Directors who give them these big guaranteed pay packages that are not tied to performance. The fact is that reported earnings are only a small piece of their income in many instances. If a person starts a company and gets stock up front, the value of that stock may not be recognized in many cases until it is actually sold. Some entrepreneurs rack up billions of dollars in wealth and report none of it in income until they sell their stock. In fact, many of today's billionaires have not paid taxes on most of their wealth accumulation. But, good for them if they came up with a new idea that developed into a valuable business.

Many people think the rich are tax cheats who don't report their full income and find ways around paying the tax they owe. I can tell you from firsthand experience, which I will discuss later, that many low income people are big tax cheaters and getting away with it every day. It's not just one group – this is a widespread issue across all income classes.

Let's discuss the top earners first. I have already mentioned how the proportion of wealth in the hands of the top 1% is increasing geometrically with 80% of the growth in wealth going to the top 1%. The spread between the rich and everyone else is widening ever more. Much of this is due to the favorable tax policies that allow them to keep more and more of their income. When people die and leave large estates there is an estate tax on the value they leave to their heirs. Currently the first $5 million is not taxed and the remainder is taxed at 35%, down from 55% just a few years ago. This was another reduction approved as part of the Bush Tax Cuts we hear so much about. In fact, if someone died during 2010 there was no estate tax. Another gift to the wealthy from George Bush. This has helped to ensure the wealthy remain so. There are other ways to pass wealth to heirs tax free such as buying large life insurance policies because the life insurance benefit is tax free to the beneficiary.

Estate Taxes

As part of the Republicans' Cut, Cap and Balance Plan proposed during the debt ceiling debate the Estate Tax would have been permanently repealed. One more way to ensure if you are rich you will remain so, as will your heirs, for years to come. We all want to find out we have a rich uncle who left us millions, so why should inheritance be taxed? Many wealthy people would say, "We already paid taxes on that money when we earned it." However the simple fact is that much of that wealth was not ever taxed. Let's assume I start a new company, call it Google, and give myself a pile of stock up-front, commonly referred to as Founders Shares. The company grows tremendously and we eventually go public, with the value of my stock growing to billions of dollars. I only pay tax on the gain on that stock if I sell it. As long as I continue to hold it I don't pay any tax on the billions of dollars by which my wealth has increased. Decades later, if I pass it on to my heirs, tax free, the wealth remains for generations without anyone paying tax on any of it (other than the few shares I sold to buy my new beach house in the Hamptons and a few dozen Ferraris and Bentleys to get me there in style). Once again, the wealth stays with the wealthy. Some Republicans, if they had their way, would permanently eliminate the inheritance tax. If this happened, the billionaires could pass their billions on to their families, untaxed for generation after generation. Oh, and by the way, when I do sell my founders shares, it would be classified as long term capital gains, taxed at only 15% under current tax law. Now if these shares were acquired through stock compensation programs which many executives get at public companies the tax would be more current and some or all of it would be ordinary income depending on when I exercise the options to buy the stock and when I sell those shares. Probably too complicated an issue to talk about here.

Income Taxes – The Bush tax Cuts

The real money in terms of the amounts received by our government is in income taxes. The big argument today is the roll back of the Bush tax cuts. Let's look at what that really means in terms of dollars. The following table compares what the federal income tax would be if we kept the tax brackets the same and simply reverted to the tax percentages for each bracket as they were before the Bush tax cuts. The brackets change constantly so I utilized the 2011 brackets and the Pre and Post Bush Tax Cut rates. Makes you wonder what all the arguments are about.

Married Filing Jointly			
Marginal Tax Rate		Tax Brackets	
Pre Bush	Post Bush	Over	But Not Over
10.0%	10.0%	$0	$16,750
15.0%	15.0%	$16,750	$68,000
27.0%	25.0%	$68,000	$137,300
30.0%	28.0%	$137,300	$209,250
35.0%	33.0%	$209,250	$373,650
38.6%	35.0%	$373,650	-

Based on these tax brackets, and the Pre and Post Bush tax cuts, the tax based on each of the following income levels and married filing jointly would be as follows:

Income	$100,000		$1,000,000	
	Pre	Post	Pre	Post
Tax Brackets				
0 - 16,750	1,675	1,675	1,675	1,675
16,750 - 68,000	7,688	7,688	7,688	7,688
68,000 - 137,300	8,640	8,000	18,711	17,325
137,300 - 209,250			21,585	20,146
209,250 - 373,650			57,540	54,252
over 373,650			241,771	219,223
Total Tax	18,003	17,363	348,970	320,308
Decrease Amount		(640)		(28,662)
Percent Decrease		-4%		-8%
Tax Rate		17%		32%

It seems pretty amazing that Congress could be hung up on a tax difference of $28,662 on a person making $1 million per year. If the tax brackets were returned to the levels they were in 2002, as well as the percentages applied to each bracket, the difference for the person making $1,000,000 is $36,451 or 3.6% of earnings. Of course, these comparisons all assume the entire income is earned income, such as salaries and earnings from a privately owned business or profession. If some of the earnings are from capital gains the total tax rate would be much lower for the person earning $1,000,000.

Does anyone really believe the successful business owner making $1,000,000 per year will stop hiring as a result of a $28 or $30 thousand difference in taxes? Let's look at this from a purely economic viewpoint.

First, let's think about why a business owner would hire a new employee in the first place. I'll give you three choices; you pick the one you think is right:

1. His tax rate is low, he has more money than he needs and he wants to do something good for his fellow man so he hires an unemployed individual out of the goodness of his heart.

2. There is an empty desk in the front office and it looks bad to customers that no one is working at it.

3. He thinks he can sell more product and therefore earn more profit, but he needs another employee to produce the product.

Well look at you, the future CEO - I'm betting you figured this one out all by yourself! John Boehner, Speaker of the House of Representatives hasn't figured it out. He's crying over how happy he is to be in a position to help the average American working family which represents 97% of the people who voted for him and probably makes on average about $45,000 per year.

So, let's look at an example (something like you would see on a high school math exam) using simple math and the answer I hope most of you picked from the choices above.

So here is Joe who manufactures widgets that he sells for $2.00 each. Each employee can produce 4,000 widgets per month or 48,000 per year. Joe's per unit cost is $1.00 per widget. He has twenty employees so Joe is happily producing 960,000 widgets per year and selling them for $1,920,000. His overhead is $700,000 and cost per employee is $35,000 or $700,000 in total. Joe is earning a pretax profit of $520,000. Yahoo! Based on this level of earnings his federal income tax is $152,308 leaving him a net of $367,692 from which he and his family of four manage to cover the basics of food, clothing, and shelter. They apparently clip a lot of coupons.

Here's where he has a big decision to make. He now feels he can sell another 30,000 widgets but he has to add one more employee to produce them at a cost of $35,000. However, the evil empire has rolled back the Bush Tax Cuts and his top tax rate is now up to 38.6% from the 35% he enjoyed earlier. If he sells 30,000 more widgets at $2.00 he earns revenue of $60,000 less the $35,000 cost of the added employee for a net additional profit of $25,000. Since the evil empire has changed the tax rates back to the pre Bush Tax Cut levels his tax will be $173,340 leaving him with $371,660 only $3,968 higher than if he hadn't hired the additional employee. His tax would have been $12,000 less if the tax rates had not been increased but they have and this is what he has to live with. If he can sell a full 48,000 more widgets he earns another $36,000 less the tax of $13,896. But for now he can only sell 30,000 more.

Let's take another quiz. Based on the facts above Joe would likely:

1. Not hire the unemployed freeloader because he doesn't want to pay more taxes even though he still ends up with $3,968 more in his pocket.

2. Fire all of his employees and say it's not worth the trouble and go on welfare.

3. Hire the additional employee, earn a net of $3,968 more and hope to fully utilize that employee with further sales in the future. (Hint, he makes more money with this option)

And your answer is.....................

Wow, I seem to have attracted a smart group of readers! I agree. He hires the additional worker in spite of the tax increases and pockets the paltry $3,968. I am still trying to figure out why so many politicians insist that tax increases will kill jobs. Sure higher taxes will stop an employer from hiring another worker if the effect of hiring is marginal or the owner's after tax net is less than he/she needs. However, if there is a market and the owner can produce and sell more products they will hire the additional worker. We have all heard about the tax increases proposed by Obama – increase taxes only on those making over $250,000. Few business owners make over $250,000, an obvious fact since only 1.5% of the total population makes this much.

The idea that reducing taxes on the rich will result in job growth is a fallacy propagated by those wishing to reduce taxes on the rich. Trickledown economics will never advance our economy. The rich get richer because the middle class, the bulk of the customers of their businesses, are buying their products. Our economy advances and the rich get richer through only one thing, other than low taxes, and that is "trickle-up economics." Consumer spending drives our economy. When the masses have money to spend, all businesses will benefit. Until they start spending money and buying products, companies will not hire more people.

It must be that very smart, hard working people become rich and then immediately forget where their wealth comes from. They are much like athletes who earn millions then forget that it's their fans, regular Americans who ultimately pay their astronomical salaries. Does anyone think Sam Walton amassed a $100 billion fortune because millionaires came into his Wal-Mart stores to buy toasters and toilet paper? Did the founders of Google earn billions because they are able to sell advertising based on the billions of millionaire eyeballs on their site every day? Absolutely not. These people earned billions because some 200 million middle class Americans patronized their businesses. The money trickled up, not down. In fact more than a trickle, it at times becomes a waterfall flowing up the cliff. As the middle class shrinks, many moving into lower class, and as we ship good paying jobs overseas, the pool of customers will continue to shrink. The founders and investors in such companies will earn less, unless they are global companies who will sell more to the increasingly affluent Chinese customer. The cycle will be self perpetuating. Add to it the need for more social programs to help the masses with no opportunity. Or, we could just let them eat dog food and sleep in cars.

This was too easy, wasn't it? But wait, could there be another side to it? This logic may work with regard to the privately owned business operating in the U.S. But what about the big multinational corporations that operate worldwide and have a choice of where to locate their companies and the jobs that go with them? Could Mr. Boehner be right in regards to them? More on that under Corporate Taxes.

So, we picked on the rich. Why shouldn't they pay more in taxes? Well, for one, they earned their money by working hard while many in our society were sitting at the bar drinking drafts purchased with welfare and unemployment checks or watching the Price is Right and cranking out too many children. Sure, some got lucky with an idea or by getting hired by the right entrepreneur who had the right or even lucky idea. But the fact is, most people who became wealthy worked very hard to earn it. Why should they have to give it to the freeloaders? Who would everyone work for if the Rockefellers, Vanderbilts, Waltons and Gates of the world didn't create their empires? These people have propelled America to the largest and strongest economy in the world. Well, it was largest and strongest at one time - now I'm not too sure. So why do the wealthy pay a disproportionate share of the taxes while 45% of the US population pays no income tax or in many cases a negative income tax? Anyone in their shoes would argue this is unfair. Let's just lay out the facts and you can decide what is fair.

Tax Distribution based on 2008 IRS Data:

Income Bracket	Income Earned	% of Total Adjusted Gross Income Reported	Percent of Total Taxes Paid	Effective Tax Rate on Income
Top 1%	$380,354+	20%	38%	23%
1% to 5%	$159,619 to $380,353	15%	21%	17%
Top 5% in Total	$159,619+	35%	58%	21%
Bottom 50%	Less than $33,048	13%	3%	2.6%

So no doubt, the rich pay a disproportionate share of the taxes compared to their percent of income. However, based on wealth, they do not pay a proportionate share. It is hard to define wealth since private citizens do not publish this information and it is nearly impossible to determine the worth of things like privately owned businesses. The available studies indicate that the top 1% wealthiest Americans hold over 35.6% of the wealth and the top 5% cumulatively holds as much as 87% of all wealth. As we mentioned earlier, much of this wealth accumulation may never have been taxed as income. Whether you believe this is fair or not, an average effective tax rate on the wealthiest 5% of Americans of only 21% is not excessive compared to other developed countries of the world. Some people will only be satisfied when they are the wealthiest person in the world. Some understand there is more. Bill Gates and Warren Buffet, who for years were the two wealthiest men in the world, understand. They are pledging and in fact have made substantial progress on giving essentially all of their approximately $100 billion of net worth to charitable causes. But others who possess wealth beyond any amount they can ever spend will fight tooth and nail to save 3% or 4% in taxes? I digress.

There can be only one reason why the wealthiest among us would or should pay a disproportionate share of income taxes. It is because we as a society have decided that each among us has a right to the basic necessities of life. Food, clothing, shelter, health care, maybe even a cheap family vacation each year. Why? Because we, as a society, have decided that those with much more than they need should voluntarily, or involuntarily, relinquish some of that excess so that others who have not had the opportunities or who were not as fortunate might live with some dignity and comfort. There are many who want to work hard but have no opportunity. Many of the 25 million unemployed today are not in such a state of their own free will or because of lack of effort. They are there because of unfortunate circumstances. They were duped into mortgages they could not understand nor afford by bankers who personally made tens of millions on their misfortune.

People lost their jobs and homes. Yes, you can say they should have known better but mommy and daddy didn't send them to private schools and hire tutors so they would do well in algebra and trigonometry. Many didn't realize they had a chance at a college education. Perhaps they did understand the risks and took only prudent risk based on their situation only to lose the job they held for 20 years because the factory closed and the company sent their job to China so a higher profit could be earned. After all, a company needs to maximize profit to support CEO and executive pay at astronomical levels; even to pay tens of millions of dollars to CEO's who turn out to be total failures.

Yes there are the freeloaders who don't want to support themselves and believe they are entitled to a free ride. And to them I say, too bad. Starve. Go without. My heart however goes out to their children, born in squalor and who will never have the guidance or resources to make anything of themselves. But do we, as a society, want to help the millions of people who work hard and make the best with what they are given but just can't seem to make it? Do we, as a society, believe the rich, who have far more than they need, or could ever spend, should be willing or be forced to pay this disproportionate share to help those who don't have enough?

Let's be honest, everyone does not have an equal chance to succeed. And in the end, everyone can't be rich. The rich got that way in many cases on the backs of low paid, hard working people. Their customers are the hard working people, many of whom do not make enough to get by on their own with the high costs of housing, food, energy and medical care.

If Sam Walton were alive today and still held his interest in Wal-Mart that has now been divided among his children he would be the richest man in the world. Incidentally, he would not have paid taxes on the vast majority of the $90 to $100 billion of wealth he would have accumulated. But the Wal-Mart empire was built on low paid employees with minimal or no health or retirement benefits. They offer limited health insurance plans offered by such companies like McDonalds which offer very minimal coverage. In many of these cases, one serious illness will bankrupt the employee with out of pocket expenses. Their customers are the same people.

Would we feel bad for Sam Walton if his wealth might have declined to $70 billion if Wal-Mart had paid its employees more and paid a larger share of better benefits? On the other hand, the U.S. is a capitalist society. One of supply and demand. These people didn't have better jobs with more pay and better benefits because they have nothing of more value to offer. Many out of laziness and many out of lack of opportunity. We have all seen many of each.

Those of us who grew up in nice homes with good families and had our college tuition paid for us can't begin to understand what it would take to rise out of a drug infested slum with shootouts in front of our homes every night and only one over-extended parent, with no education and no money, and make it to college so that we would one day command more value in the marketplace.

Notice that I have provided no answer offered so far, just questions. However I believe that we, as a nation, by developing social programs like unemployment compensation, workers compensation, college loan programs, education grants, Social Security and Medicare, as well as a progressive federal income tax system, answered the question a long time ago. We do believe we should take more from those who have too much and give to those who don't have enough. This only leaves the questions of: How much is too much? How much is too little? Should those with too little get more if they don't even try to fend for themselves? Where should we draw the line?

Essentially every other developed country in the world has addressed this issue also and deals with the same questions. They also have too little to go around. Or at least their governments have too little to go around. Some provide a higher level of social services than the U.S. and some provide less. Essentially every one has a higher income tax than the

U.S. The chart above shows the U.S. tax rate at 28% of GDP is 20% lower than the average of several of the largest economies among the OECD countries. Let's look at the maximum tax rate in these countries for personal income taxes.

	GDP	Top Marginal Tax Tate
	In trillions	
United States	14.70	35%
China	10.10	45%
Japan	4.30	50%
India	4.00	30%
Germany	2.90	45%
Russia	2.20	13%
United Kingdom	2.20	50%
Brazil	2.10	27.50%
France	2.10	40%
Italy	1.80	43%
Average		38%
Weighted Average		39%

The weighted average is simply the average of all the listed countries weighted based on the size of the GDP. For example a country with a GDP of 4.0 trillion counts for twice as much toward the average as a country with a GDP of 2.0 trillion.

India and Russia are lower than us. I think we have an idea how the poor live in these countries, especially India. Maybe eating dirt isn't so bad if you have a little ketchup to put on it. The US rate is only 3% below the average, or 4% below the weighted average. Increasing the personal tax rate to the average would require a 10% tax increase which equates to about $100 billion in additional revenue to the U.S. Government. A small piece of the deficit, but a step in the right direction. The real measure is the total tax rate and as I stated earlier, even the top 1% only pay tax at 23%, nowhere near the top rate. The reasons are the myriad of tax credits and deductions, nontaxable growth in wealth and lower rates of tax for capital gains. The capital gains tax is perhaps the biggest loophole for the wealthy. Capital gains, gains on the sale of investments such as stocks, bonds and real estate, are taxed at only 15% regardless of your overall tax rate. For the super wealthy, capital gains are generally one of their largest, and frequently the largest, source of income. Taxing these gains at very low rates represents a tremendous tax benefit to the small minority who hold the greatest percentage of these assets. This treatment goes a long way toward ensuring that the rich continue to accumulate a larger and larger piece of the total wealth in America. Some increase in the top rate may be in order but we also must consider the tax rates for everyone in between.

We can look at one actual example to put the capital gains tax issue in perspective. In 2010, presidential candidate Mitt Romney and his wife earned $21 million, mostly from investments. He also listed a number of offshore investments, likely in funds sheltered from U.S. income taxes. Their tax rate was 13.9%. Let's compare that to a working couple with no children. First, if their income was from salaries they would pay 7.65% for Social Security and Medicare taxes if we exclude the effect of the temporary 2% reduction in Social Security tax. Including the taxpayers share tax of Social Security Tax, in order to pay a total of 15% tax they could earn a total of $50,000. Excluding the Social Security tax they could earn $120,000 in order to pay a 15% tax. So in this case Mitt would have earned 400 times as much as our average couple and paid the same overall tax rate. What a sweet deal. No wonder the nation's richest people are contributing millions to get him elected.

Income Taxes – Low Income Taxpayers

Let's talk about taxes on the lower class individuals within our society. Here is where most people have no clue what is happening. If you pay income taxes and do not want to become angry, skip this section. Late in 2010 I relocated back to Scranton, PA. I am a CPA so I went to work for one of the big tax preparation chains for the first few months of 2011 preparing personal tax returns, mainly for low income people. I saw much of this first hand.

A little primer. The U.S. Tax Code has a few sweet items in it for low income people, especially those with children. The biggest ones are:

1. Child Tax Credit – A credit of $1,000 for each qualifying child under age 17. This is a pure credit, not a reduction in taxable income and is generally paid to the person even if their income tax is zero.

    a. A qualifying child is a biological child, legally adopted child, foster child, brother, sister, step sister or step brother or a descendent of them.

2. Earned Income Credit – A direct credit based on earned income also paid to the taxpayer even if their income tax is zero. It mainly benefits people with children. Similarly qualifying children as the Child Tax Credit above but children under 19 or under 24 and full time student qualify. Even nieces and nephews qualify. If your earned income is very low, so is the credit. As your income increases so does the credit to a point then it begins to reverse

again until it goes back to zero. If you have no children it disappears at $13,400 of earned income but at much higher levels if the taxpayer has children. The numbers involved will surprise you.

The poor, uneducated people who came into our offices certainly knew how to work the system. They were well educated when it came to knowing how to answer questions to maximize these credits.

Let's look at two actual examples.

1. A young woman in her mid twenties comes to my desk. She has two children, each with last names different than hers. As part of the due diligence required for the Earned Income Credit I have to ask about the other parent of the children. One is in prison, whereabouts of the other unknown. Here is how her 2010 tax return looks:

Tax Calcualtion

Earned Income (Wages)	$ 16,000
Standard Deduction - Head of Household	(8,350)
Personal exemptions (3 x 3,650)	(10,950)
Taxable income	(3,300)
Income Tax	**ZERO**
Credits	
Tax Withheld From Pay	1,900
Making Work Pay Credit	400
Earned Income Credit	5,000
Child Tax Credit	2,000
Total Credits	9,300
Refund Amount	**$ 9,300**

So out of the $9,300 refund, a total of $7,400 was due entirely to government credits simply given to the taxpayer. Remember, this is a paid credit, not income, so it will never be included in taxable income.

Let's look at one that is infinitely more egregious. I am not making this up; it is based on a real case. A couple walks in the door with one of their three children. The child is around 12 years old. They do not speak English so she is the translator. Think they don't know what they are doing? Think again. Here is the situation:

They are not U.S. Citizens. They are resident aliens working in the U.S. They appear to be Russian or Ukrainian based on their names and accents. They claim to be unmarried but have three children together and live together. The man earns $17,000 and the woman earns $10,000. If they were married filing jointly they would have $27,000 of earned income and three children to claim as exemptions. Ignoring their tax withholding their refund from the Earned Income Credit and Child Tax Credit would be as follows:

Earned Income Credit	$3,427
Child Tax Credit	$3,000
Total Refund from Credits	$6,427

But I told you these people know what they are doing. They come in and claim that they are not married and want to file separate returns. So what's the difference? Read, then weep.

	Man	Woman	Combined
Earned Income	$17,000	$10,000	$27,000
# Children Claimed	2	1	3
Earned Income Credit	$4,901	$3,043	$7,944
Child Tax Credit	$2,000	$1,000	$3,000
Total Credits (Refund)	$6,901	$4,043	$10,944

So by what may or may not have been lying about their marital status, their refund went from $6,427 to $10,944, an increase of $4,517. Based on their earnings, his income tax is $135 but zero after the Making Work Pay Credit of $400. Her income tax is zero also. So these people walk out with a free check for $10,944 compliments of the taxpayers of the United States and they aren't even U.S. citizens. Remember it's a tax refund so it isn't taxable income next year either. It's a free and clear gift. No wonder everyone wants to come to America.

I saw cases like this every day. It infuriated me. What's even worse is the entitlement attitude these people have about it. They feel it is owed to them. Don't think for a moment it's only the rich who cheat on their taxes. These people whose income tax is zero are also cheating. The level of dishonesty is high because of this entitlement mentality. Some of the ways they cheat:

A man and a woman come in and the woman has no income. She lives with the man and has a child. He claims the child is his stepson. I ask a few questions like "How is this child your stepson? Are you married to her?" The answer is no so I tell them the child does not qualify for Earned Income Credit.

They argue that they got it last year. Yes, I tell them, but they were not entitled to it. They get mad and walk out and go over to the other tax preparation service where some yahoo with three weeks of tax training is doing returns and knows nothing about this and they now claim the child is his stepson or nephew or that they are married and they get the EIC.

I have had several clients tell me that people at their work were selling their children's Social Security numbers. If someone's income was very low for the year and they knew their EIC would be low, they would sell their child's information. People then go to the tax preparer with the Social Security card in hand and claim it as their child or some family member's child who they support. They have all the answers rehearsed. The U.S. pays about $40 billion per year in Earned Income Credit and although I do not have a valid statistical analysis, based on my firsthand experience, over 10% of that is potentially fraudulent. However the bigger issue is the amounts we are paying people for having children. It can be a pretty profitable venture if you don't spend too much on the children. These people are being rewarded for being totally irresponsible. I remember a young Hispanic woman came to our office to file her return. She was only 25 or 26. She had three young children, all with different last names, none of the fathers in the picture and less than $6,000 in earnings. Of course she walks out with $6,000 as a reward for having babies she can't possibly support.

So while 45% of the population pays no tax, a big percentage of those are walking away with big checks coming their way due to these credit programs. Why do so many pay zero income tax? Well you start with your earned income (wages and business income) plus investment, pension and other income, of which most of these people have none. Then, for married filing jointly, for 2011, you get a standard deduction of $11,600 and an exemption amount of $3,700 for each person. The standard deduction and exemption amounts increase every year. So a family of four needs to make $26,000 before they owe one dollar of tax. And of course that would be more than offset by the credits.

In fact, after considering Child Tax Credit and Earned Income Credits, but assuming they qualify for none of the other credits available, a family of four would need to earn over $45,400 before they would owe $1 of Federal Income Tax.

Income Taxes – Middle Class

Let's shift gears and zero in on the "average American," the middle class. We'll look at two income scenarios, both married filing jointly, with two children each. One family has income of $65,000, the other an income of $100,000. Let's also assume they don't claim any other of the myriad of other credits such as education credit for tuition paid for college, deduction for student loan interest, credit for retirement savings including money put into a 401K at work or credit for child care expenses if both spouses work. Of course in at least the second case they probably own a home and have itemized deductions greater than the $11,600 standard deduction assumed, which would further lower their tax, but let's just ignore that. What do their taxes based on 2011 tax rates look like?

	$65,000	$100,000
Total Income (AGI)	$65,000	$100,000
Less:		
Standard Deduction	11,600	11,600
Personal Exemptions	14,800	14,800
	26,400	26,400
Taxable Income	38,600	73,600
Income tax	4,944	10,656
Credits:		
Earned Income Credit	-	-
Child Tax Credit	2,000	2,000
	2,000	2,000
Net Income Tax	**2,944**	**8,656**
Income Tax as % of AGI	**4.5%**	**8.7%**
Add Other taxes:		
Social Security Tax	4,030	6,200
Medicare Tax	943	1,450
Total Income & Other Tax	**7,917**	**16,306**
Total % of AGI	**12.2%**	**16.3%**

These percentages are not in any way egregious, in fact, I'm sure many of you are shocked to see such low percentages. A family of four making $100,000 has income tax of only 8.7% of income and total tax including Social Security and Medicare of only 16.3% of income. We all know there is a tremendous amount of government waste, but there is also a great deal of services provided from our tax dollars. Everyone thinks $1 of tax is too much, but we must remember these funds do not go entirely to entitlement programs for the poor and unemployed but also for our own Social Security, transportation, defense, federal government, and a host of other vital services.

Government Projected Tax Revenue

With Congress trying to plan for the future and evaluate future deficits going forward, you would hope they are using credible information.   Our government annually prepares budget projections going out a number of years.   They base policy decisions, mainly dealing with spending and tax revenue on these projections. The Congressional Budget Office prepared an analysis of the President's latest budget, and I found one thing of particular interest.   The projection goes out much farther but the following are the projected tax revenues through 2016.

	Actual						% increase
	2010	2011	2012	2013	2014	2015	2010 to 2015
	In billions of dollars						
Revenues							
Individual income taxes	899	998	1,128	1,517	1,669	1,822	102.7%
Corporate income taxes	191	201	279	343	427	395	106.5%
Social insurance taxes	865	818	942	1,027	1,090	1,147	32.7%
Other revenues	208	213	210	200	254	278	33.8%
Total Revenues	2,163	2,230	2,558	3,087	3,440	3,642	68.4%

Where might they have come up with the assumption (and how can they be managing our country under the assumption) that individual and corporate income taxes are going to double over the next five years? If the unemployment rate falls back to normal levels of 4% to 5%, that would mean 4% more people working – certainly a far cry from double the number of people working. Furthermore, I submit that while it would be economically advantageous to those people put back to work, because of our ridiculous tax system, it could actually cost the U.S. Government money if more people get jobs. Let's look at a not unrealistic scenario.

Assume eight million unemployed people suddenly get jobs. Assume they are not currently receiving unemployment as many unemployed have long ago exhausted those benefits. Look at two assumptions – one where their average wage is $9.00 per hour and another where their average wage is $12.00 per hour. Low paying yes but not unrealistic given the shortage of good paying jobs available today. Let's further assume each is married and has two children. Utilizing 2011 tax rates their net tax for all eight million people would look like this:

Hourly Rate		$9.00		$12.00
Total Earnings	$	18,000	$	24,000
Less:				
Standard deduction		11,600		11,600
Personal exemptions		14,800		14,800
Taxable income		(8,400)		(2,400)
Income Tax		-		-
Employee Share of Social Security & Medicare Tax		1,377		1,836
Employer Share of Social Security & Medicare Tax		1,377		1,836
Total of all taxes		2,754		3,672
Credits:				
Earned Income Credit		4,831		3,567
Child Tax Credit		2,000		2,000
		6,831		5,567
Net tax per taxpayer		(4,077)		(1,895)
Total loss on 8,000,000 taxpayers	$	(32,616,000,000)	$	(15,160,000,000)

No further comment offered nor required.

One alternative offered to alleviate the inequities in taxes is a flat tax or one with a big federal sales tax. Some propose the elimination of the capital gains tax. Make no mistake about it, a flat tax or a federal sales tax in place of income tax, especially with the capital gains tax eliminated, is another big tax cut for the rich and a tax increase for all lower and middle class families. The rich spend a far lower percent of their income than the middle class who typically spend all or substantially all of their income and therefore a sales tax would hit them much harder. Why is it that some Republicans want to exclude capital gains from taxable income? Why isn't that considered income to them? They will claim it incentivizes people to invest and therefore provide needed capital to companies so they can grow and hire more people. Unfortunately, many people in America are buying that fallacy.

Part III

Corporate Income Taxes

Don't be scared by the heading. We won't be delving into the details of the incredibly complex world of corporate taxes. But it is important for taxpayers to understand the macro issues. Here too, the laws are bought and paid for by the rich and powerful. Why should you care about corporate taxes? Because when the large corporations don't pay their share the government only has one other source to look to in order to make up the shortfall – YOU! Corporate taxes are relatively small compared to personal income taxes. In 2011 income tax revenue to the U.S. Government was split as follows:

	(In billions)
Personal Income Taxes	$998
Corporate Income Taxes	$201
Social Insurance Taxes	$818 – paid half by the employee and half by the employer

U.S. Corporations constantly complain that the corporate income tax rate is too high so many have moved operations to other countries where taxes are lower or nonexistent. This has resulted in the loss of jobs in the U.S. and the loss of tax revenue.

The largest U.S. corporations seldom pay anywhere near the 35% maximum tax rate. As a result of myriad special tax credits, exclusions and provisions buried in the thousands of pages of tax code, and the impact of these big corporations moving profitable operations to countries with low tax rates outside the U.S., many of them pay no income taxes at all. It is almost impossible to evaluate what they should be paying in taxes in the U.S. The question becomes how much of their profit is attributable to U.S. business (which should be the fair basis for the taxes that they pay). Determining this can be extremely complicated and these companies have armies of accounting and tax experts figuring out ways to minimize taxes. Earnings in foreign countries are not taxed in the U.S. until the profits are brought into the U.S., resulting in many large corporations keeping large sums of money offshore in an effort to avoid paying taxes on those earnings. Some large corporations specifically move profitable operations to low tax areas to avoid taxes. Many of the largest corporations have paid no taxes to the U.S. over the past several years despite billions in earnings.

Many articles have been written explaining how companies making billions are receiving tax refunds from the U.S. How can that be? One article says that these companies are paying no taxes and another says they are paying more than the maximum marginal tax rate. This is not meant to be a detailed discussion on corporate taxes. These taxes, especially involving large corporations, are incredibly complex. General Electric, one of the largest corporations in the world and the current poster child for U.S. tax avoidance has a tax department of 975 employees. An overview to allow everyone to understand the basics is in order so let's sort this out briefly before you fall asleep.

First, there are many kinds of taxes:

- Income taxes – taxes paid based on the profit of the corporation. On corporate financial statements they will appear as:
  - Current taxes – those actually paid to the taxing authorities
  - Deferred taxes – Taxes accrued based on income reported in financial statements but due to tax law differences may not yet be payable. An example might be where

an asset is depreciated over 10 years on the financial statements but depreciated over five years for taxes resulting in a higher book income than taxable income.

- Sales Taxes – same tax we all pay when we purchase an item that is not for resale.
- VAT – (Value Added Tax) These charges exist in essentially every country other than the U.S. Think of it as a sales tax but only on the increase in value of an item by the company paying it. What does that mean? Suppose a company buys a piece of steel for $100. They then form it into a part and it is now worth $150. The value added is $50 so when they sell it they would pay a tax on the increase in value. So a 10% VAT would cost them $5.00 in this example ($50 increase in value times 10%).

So, while we hear of companies paying little or no income taxes they may be paying many of these other taxes. However, these other taxes are already taken into account in computing income so the focus of the ire is on the income taxes paid by these companies.

One other reason a corporation may not pay tax or even get a refund in a year of high profits is because of what's called a net operating loss carry forward. If a company loses a lot of money in one year they can carry that loss forward to future years to offset income. It is only fair as this is part of the cost of doing business. It in effect looks at earnings over several years so taxes are paid over time based on the average rate of earnings. By the way, if you or I own a business and lose money one year we can do the same on our personal returns.

The organization Citizens for Tax Justice (www.ctj.org) did an analysis of the twelve largest tax avoiding corporations in the US. They looked at their profits and taxes for 2008, 2009 and 2010. The companies included GE, DuPont, American Electric Power, Verizon, Boeing, Wells Fargo, FedEx, Honeywell, IBM, Yahoo, United Technologies and Exxon Mobil. Over this three year period, these companies had profits attributable to U.S. business of $171 billion and received a net tax refund of $2.5 billion, resulting in a negative 1.5% tax rate! That's a long way from the 35% tax rate these corporations are complaining is too high for them to make a profit. Had they paid tax at the full rate of 35% the tax revenues to the U.S. would have been $60 billion. Obviously something is wrong with the U.S. Corporate Tax Code. These companies accomplish this through special tax credits they get by lobbying congress and making big donations. They also result from net operating loss carry forwards, special tax treatment on specific items, and many other special provisions the "bought and paid for" members of Congress bestow upon them. The tax law changes have resulted in a decline of revenue from corporate taxes from 30% in the 1950's to less than 10% of Federal tax revenue today.

Let's look briefly at GE. From 2005 to 2009 GE had profits attributable to its U.S. business of $26 billion and received tax refunds from the IRS totaling $4 billion. How do they earn billions and pay taxes averaging about 7.4% of U.S. profits over longer periods of time? The actual taxes paid are even less (actually negative) than that because this includes taxes that will be paid only if foreign profits are brought back to the U.S. How do they do it?

One way is through special tax credits. GE spends millions of dollars per year to lobby for changes in tax law, from more generous depreciation schedules on jet engines they build and lease, to green energy credits for its wind turbines.

Their biggest tax strategy is moving profits to countries where they pay no taxes. One of the biggest parts of GE is not the company making any products but its financial arm involved in lending and leasing which accounts for 30% of its revenue. In the late 1990's, G.E. and other financial services firms won a change in tax law that allowed them and other multinational lending and leasing companies to avoid taxes on some banking income. The change meant that if G.E. financed the sale of a jet engine in another country, they would no longer have to pay U.S. tax on the interest income as long as the profits remained offshore. This tax break allowed G.E. to avoid taxes on lending income from abroad, and permitted the company to amass tax credits, write-offs and depreciation. Those benefits are then used to offset taxes on its American manufacturing profits.

Was this strategy bought and paid for? You decide. When Congress threatened to let the loophole expire in 2008 GE worked with lobbyists to ensure it would be renewed. They met with Representative Charles Rangel, then chairman of the Ways and Means Committee, which would decide the fate of the tax break. Mr. Rangel soon reversed his opposition to the tax break. The following month Mr. Immelt, the CEO of GE announced that its foundation had awarded $30 million to New York City schools, including $11 million to benefit various schools in Mr. Rangel's district.

Today, U.S. business accounts for 46% of GE's revenue and 18% of its profits. GE would argue that the U.S. benefits from its success. How have we benefitted? Well, we receive essentially no tax revenue from them, over the past ten years, the percent of their revenue and profit from foreign sources has skyrocketed, and they have laid off 20% of their U.S. workforce. Wow, thank you very much, GE!

This is so much fun let's look at one more. Google saves about $1 billion per year by moving its profit to foreign subsidiaries. How? They develop their software and processes, referred to as intellectual property in the US. They then license it to a subsidiary called Google Ireland Holdings. It is an Irish company, but is managed in Bermuda, exempting it from tax in Ireland. Google Ireland receives the revenue from all of Google's sales outside the U.S. It then pays almost all of that to the Bermuda company as a licensing fee for the intellectual property leaving only a minimal profit in the Irish company. Incidentally, there is no corporate income tax in Bermuda. So what has Google accomplished? They created a product in the U.S., derived tremendous amounts of revenue from it and funneled the profits to Bermuda eliminating almost all income tax.

A New York Times article by David Leonhardt stated the following:

Of the 500 big companies in the well-known Standard & Poor's stock index, 115 paid a total corporate tax rate — both federal and otherwise — of less than 20 percent over the last five years, according to an analysis of company reports done for The New York Times by Capital IQ, a research firm. Thirty-nine of those companies paid a rate less than 10 percent.

Arguably, the United States now has a corporate tax code that's the worst of all worlds. The official rate is higher than in almost any other country, which forces companies to devote enormous time and effort to finding loopholes.

Some people claim we should lower or even eliminate corporate taxes as that will create jobs. Does anyone really believe that if we reduced the corporate tax rates these companies will run out and hire millions of people? Go back to my earlier quiz on why companies hire people. Will they conclude that their tax rate is low so they should go out and hire more employees even if there is no associated increase in revenue? Of course not. Or, would they hire only if they can generate more profit? Greed knows no boundaries. Money creates a demand for more money and lower taxes will change nothing. Yes they have to be competitive but do they really need a tax rate at 7% in order to compete in the global economy?

There is a complication when dealing with large multinational corporations. The corporate entity and their management have just one goal, to maximize shareholder value. Are they not abiding by that when they move operations to countries with lower tax rates? They still have to pay U.S. taxes on their operations in the U.S. But why not locate your subsidiary doing business in Europe in Ireland where taxes are lower? Companies are doing it and costing the U.S. tens of billions of dollars per year in tax revenue and moving jobs to those companies. They are not screwing America; they are doing what is right for their shareholders. We as a nation must come up with a way to make America as attractive a place for these big companies to do business in as other countries.

Corporate income tax in the U.S. as a percent of GDP has declined steadily. In 1952 it stood at 6.1%. In 2010 that number was 1.1% and in 2011 1.9%. Measurement against GDP is important because it relates it to the volume of goods and services produced and therefore against the size of our economy. To put this in dollar terms, at 1.9% in 2011 corporate taxes were $201 billion. Had they been at the same percent of GDP as in 1952, a change I am not proposing, they would have been $645 billion.

Many companies are doing what GE and Google are doing, moving operations and even corporate headquarters to countries with lower tax rates. This is costing the U.S. tens of billions of dollars per year in tax revenue and moving jobs to other countries. Ireland has become a second Silicon Valley with tremendous growth in high tech companies. How is it that Ireland can support itself with a 12.5% corporate income tax while the U.S. cannot with a 35% corporate tax rate? Several reasons.

U.S. companies seldom pay anywhere near the 35% rate due to movement of operations to other countries and the many tax credits and special provisions that allow them to be taxed at much lower rates. Ireland makes up for it in other ways: Higher personal income tax and Value Added Taxes

The main area where the U.S. could make up this difference is in personal income taxes. As stated earlier, the U.S. is under taxed compared to other developed countries. Even Warren Buffet, one of the world's richest men with a net worth of around $50 billion agrees. On August 15, 2011 he made the following statements:

>"My friends and I have been coddled long enough by a billionaire-friendly Congress. It's time for our government to get serious about shared sacrifice,"

Buffett, one of the world's richest men and chairman of conglomerate Berkshire Hathaway Inc. said his federal tax bill last year was $6,938,744. "That sounds like a lot of money. But what I paid was only 17.4 percent of my taxable income - and that's actually a lower percentage than was paid by any of the other 20 people in our office. Their tax burdens ranged from 33 percent to 41 percent and averaged 36 percent," he said.

Buffett said higher taxes for the rich will not discourage investment. "I have worked with investors for 60 years and I have yet to see anyone - not even when capital gains rates were 39.9 percent in 1976 - 77 shy away from a sensible investment because of the tax rate on the potential gain," he said "People invest to make money, and potential taxes have never scared them off."

His tax is so low because like most wealthy people much or most of his income comes from capital gains taxed at just 15%. Apparently we believe he needs these tax breaks because, well, $40 billion just wouldn't be enough.

Let's specifically look at Ireland, a country that is taking our jobs by the thousands. Not because they are doing anything wrong, it's just that their government is apparently smarter than ours. Their system helps to maintain a smaller wealth and income gap. In the U.S. the top 1% takes home 24% of the income versus 7.9% in Ireland. The top 1% in Ireland control 20% of the country's wealth while in the U.S., the top 1% controls 35%. The quest for more and more wealth in the U.S., supported by our Government, has hampered our ability to make fundamentally important decisions that could help to move us out of the dire economic and debt situation we are in. This country cannot move forward without a sound economic policy. Ireland is getting our good paying jobs while we wallow in partisan bickering and protection of special interests in Washington D.C. Ireland is creating an environment where corporations want to go and take their jobs with them because their people are all contributing more to making it an attractive destination. Here is how a person's income tax would differ between the U.S. and Ireland.

Ireland's personal income tax for a married couple is 20% on the first 45,400 Euros (about $65,600 USD) and 41% on the rest. In addition, capital gains are taxed at 25%. This is considerably higher than the U.S. and results in a more even distribution and in the ability to attract large corporations and the jobs they bring. Let's look at comparable tax returns.

Situation one – Salary based income of $45,000, married filing jointly with one child:

		U.S.		Ireland
Income	$	45,000	$	45,000
Standard Deduction & Exemptions		(22,350)		–
Taxable Income		22,650		45,000
Income tax		2,559		9,000
Child Tax Credit		(1,000)		
Total Tax		1,559		9,000
Percent of Income		3.5%		20.0%

Situation two – Salary of $500,000 and $100,000 capital gains

		U.S.		Ireland
Salaries	$	500,000	$	500,000
Capital Gains		100,000		100,000
Standard Deduction & Exemptions		(22,350)		–
Taxable Income on Ordinary Income		477,650		500,000
Income Tax on Ordinary Income		130,421		191,224
Tax on Capital gains		15,000		25,000
Total Tax		145,421		216,224
Tax - % of Total Income		24.2%		36.0%

In this case the personal income tax is 50% higher in Ireland. This explains how Ireland can afford a much lower corporate tax rate and attract companies. The personal taxes support it and the addition of jobs helps create more personal income tax through higher employment. Why can't we do this in the U.S? Because 5% of the population needs $9,000 coats and $1,000 shoes. Because the rich, who are already overwhelmingly rich need more, the poor need to be rewarded for their irresponsibility and those in the middle actually enjoy a rather low overall income tax rate.

I read an interesting article on msnbc.com by Brian Alexander in which he discusses a study by Dacher Keltner, a professor of psychology at the University of California, Berkeley. In it he refers to a study by Keltner who says the rich really are different, and not in a good way: Their life experience makes them less empathetic, less altruistic, and generally more selfish. Keltner argues that "upper-class rank perceptions trigger a focus away from the context toward the self...." In other words, rich people are more likely to think about themselves. "They think that economic success and political outcomes, and personal outcomes, have to do with individual behavior, a good work ethic," said Keltner. Because the rich gloss over the ways family connections, money and education helped, they come to denigrate the role of government and vigorously oppose taxes to fund it.

In the current presidential campaign Mitt Romney is working to convince people that he did not inherit and made his many millions totally on his own. He earned an undergraduate degree from Brigham Young and a Law degree and an MBA from Harvard. Do you suppose he graduated with a pile of student loans? His father was a famous auto industry CEO and Governor of Michigan. Dad fronted the money for Mitt's first house. No doubt his father provided him a Rolodex of contacts most others would give their right arm to have. Not taking away from his success, but to be talking like he rose from the ashes and was totally self made is nothing but senseless babble. Is it believable that if he were born to a single mother with no education living in poverty that his life would have turned out the same? Why not just admit you were born with a silver spoon in our mouth, with advantages most other people could only dream of? This denial is the view of many successful people, most of whom had some head start in life.

We do need the wealthy to create the companies that others work for and invest in. We need their companies to generate the products and advancements that make our lives better. But they need everyone else also to be the consumers for their companies, to work in their companies and to be their fellow citizens. The rich can only survive by suppressing those who oppose them or by sharing some of the wealth. Some spreading of the wealth may result in a reduction in a whole host of social ills such as mental distress, drug abuse, infant mortality, ever increasing health issues and crime.

Governments in Egypt, Libya, Syria and others are coming to learn what happens when the good of the many is sacrificed for the excesses of the few. Not that we can expect rioting in the streets and an overthrow of the U.S. Government. That would be all but impossible. However, the decline of our society certainly can be an outcome. As we send more and more jobs overseas and eliminate work in the U.S., we may be creating a giant class of perpetually poor citizens with no hope for the future. When a large portion of the population has no hope, the fabric of society declines. Crime will certainly increase as more people have nothing to lose. The need for and cost of social programs increases. Who will buy the products produced by American companies? Put yourself in the position of seeing your children hungry. What wouldn't you do to solve that?

This all points to one conclusion: as a result of special tax provisions added at the behest of America's largest and most powerful corporations, the most profitable companies in America pay well less than the stated tax rates. Many highly profitable companies consistently pay federal income tax rates in single or near single digits. Their multibillion dollar incomes are frequently taxed at rates consistent with those of individuals in the lowest tax brackets. Reform is definitely in order.

CHAPTER III

HEALTH CARE SYSTEM

First point, health insurance companies don't care about you or anyone else. They are like every other corporation, formed to maximize shareholder wealth and enrich their executives. Keep this in mind as you read this chapter.

There are two ways to obtain health insurance in the U.S.

First: You can participate in a group plan, generally offered through your employer. In this situation, there is typically no underwriting and you are usually guaranteed to be accepted at a standard rate. Underwriting is the process whereby the health insurers evaluate the risk to decide whether to accept you as a policyholder. In the case of health insurance, that will involve reviewing a health questionnaire you fill out with your medical history. They may even request medical records from your prior doctor. Groups escape this process because the insurer is somewhat guaranteed a "normal" group because everyone participates. They generally require that a certain percentage of employees participate to ensure this and protect against anti selection – the practice where only the sick buy a policy.

Second: You can buy an individual policy. This is generally more expensive and diligently underwritten by the insurer. If you have ever taken an aspirin they will probably decline you. In fairness to the obtuse individuals who run these companies, they do this because individuals frequently go without health insurance until something happens. Then, when they know they are sick with something serious, they want to run out and buy a policy. This results in far higher costs for the insurance company due to this anti selection. On the other end of the spectrum, they sometimes decline applicants for ridiculous reasons.

When the new health care legislation was passed, two provisions were most contentious. Those were the provisions that said every person was required to buy health insurance and the requirement that insurers accept you regardless of preexisting conditions. Unfortunately it didn't say how much they could charge you. So, if you have a preexisting condition you can buy health insurance but you better be Warren Buffett's long lost stepchild if you want to be able to afford it. Here are the most important provisions of the bill; summarized because the legislation is over 1,000 pages and no one read it all before they voted.

Health Insurance Exchanges will be created: The uninsured and self-employed would be able to purchase insurance through state-based exchanges with subsidies available to individuals and families with income between the 133 percent and 400 percent of poverty level. The current poverty level is $14,570 for a family of two and $22,050 for a family of four. Separate exchanges would be created for small businesses to purchase coverage -- effective 2014.

Medicare:

- Closes the Medicare prescription drug "donut hole" by 2020. Seniors who hit the donut hole by 2010 will receive a $250 rebate.

  - The donut hole is essentially a gap in coverage for prescription drugs. Under the Medicare prescription drug plan, you pay up to the first $310 of your drug costs. This is the deductible. Thereafter, you pay a copayment and your Part D drug plan pays the rest for each drug until your combined amount (including your deductible) reaches $2840. You will then be in the donut hole. You get a 50% discount on covered brand-name prescription medications but you pay the full amount yourself. The donut hole continues until your total out-of-pocket cost reaches $4,550. This annual out-of-pocket spending amount includes your yearly deductible, copayment, and coinsurance amounts.

Medicaid:

- Expands Medicaid to include 133 percent of the federal poverty level which is $29,327 for a family of four.
- Requires states to expand Medicaid to include childless adults starting in 2014.
- Federal Government pays 100 percent of costs for covering newly eligible individuals through 2016.
- Illegal immigrants are not eligible for Medicaid.

Insurance Reforms:

- Six months after enactment, insurance companies could no longer deny children coverage based on a preexisting condition.
- Starting in 2014, insurance companies cannot deny coverage to anyone with preexisting conditions.

- Insurance companies must allow children to stay on their parent's insurance plans until age 26th.

Individual Mandate: In 2014, everyone must purchase health insurance or face a $695 annual fine. There are some exceptions for low-income people. This provision has been stricken down in court and it will now be decided by the Supreme Court.

Employer Mandate: Employers with more than 50 employees must provide health insurance or pay a fine of $2000 per worker each year if any worker receives federal subsidies to purchase health insurance. Fines are applied to the entire number of employees minus some allowances. There is also a tax credit to help small companies pay for employee health insurance.

Illegal Immigrants: Illegal immigrants will not be allowed to buy health insurance in the exchanges -- even if they pay completely with their own money.

In order to pay for the expanded coverage: Starting in 2012, the Medicare tax is raised to 2.35% from 1.45% for individuals earning more than $200,000 and married couples with incomes over $250,000. The tax is imposed on some investment income for that income group. Also, beginning in 2018, insurance companies will pay a 40 percent excise tax on so-called "Cadillac" high-end health insurance plans worth over $27,500 for families ($10,200 for individuals).

Since so many people are losing coverage from their employers due to high unemployment, affordable and reasonable coverage must be made available to individuals. The new health insurance exchanges enacted as part of the health care reform may help. However, if you are not below the stated multiples of the poverty level, it may be difficult. Getting an individual policy today is nearly impossible due to the stupidity of the insurance companies and their desire to minimize the sale of individual policies. I presume this is due to the anti selection risk mentioned above. Let me relay what I went through when I tried to buy an individual policy.

> I applied to every major health insurance company in California in 2009. I was declined by every one except Kaiser Permanente. Blue Shield went to the point of requesting medical records from my doctor then sent me a letter explaining why I was denied. Here are the four reasons I was declined, then I will explain the insanity of it.
>
> 1. Cellulitis of the toe with paronychia in the last three years
>
> 2. Insomnia treated with medication

3. Low back pain with disk herniations with... with orthopedic referral

4. Elevated cholesterol, no treatment noted; conditions requiring Lisinopril and Prilosec

You decide if I should be denied coverage from every major carrier. Here is my explanation on each of the above and why declination was ridiculous.

1. This ailment was a pain in my big toe. The doctor looked at it and said I should grow the toenail out a little and be sure to cut it straight across. Definitely a reason for declination.

2. I, like probably 95% of the people reading this sometimes have trouble sleeping. I was given a prescription for Ambien, a very common prescription. If they looked at the frequency of the prescriptions they would have seen that I took it about twice per month. Again, a definite reason to decline me.

3. This one is a little more serious. As a result of a pinched nerve I had a steroid injection in a lower back disk about two and a half years before they declined me. There was no further recurrence or treatment required.

4. This last one irritates me the most. If you are big and fat with cholesterol through the roof and blood pressure boiling over, you can get coverage as long as you don't do anything about it. I was responsible and had these tested and took some common medications to control them. Both my cholesterol and blood pressure were well within accepted ranges as a result of the medication I was on. Although it's hard to estimate, the Centers for Disease Control estimate that 11 million Americans are on cholesterol drugs. They estimate another 25 million should be. Based on that, about 10% of the U.S. population is walking around with high cholesterol and would probably be allowed to buy individual health insurance even though they are ticking time bombs. My cholesterol and blood pressure were well controlled with a relatively inexpensive drug but because I was responsible about it and took care of myself I was a bad risk and denied coverage.

I was eating well, going to the gym regularly, and otherwise lived a pretty safe lifestyle. If I couldn't get health insurance, who could? While I am not wildly in favor of trying to force people to buy health insurance, I sure support the notion that some changes are in order.

The unfortunate thing is that the health care reform acts did not address the most important issues facing our health care system today: cost. We in the U.S. spend more on health care than any other developed nation, yet we do not, by most measures, have the best quality of care. Let's look at a few statistics presented by the Organisation for Economic Co-operation and Development (OECD). There are 34 member countries of the OECD mostly comprised of Europe, Scandinavia and North America. They released data on member countries' health care costs and results. Here are some interesting statistics on the largest developed countries within the OECD membership:

Country	Life Expectancy	Infant Mortality (per 1,000)	Per Capita Health Expenditures	Percent of Health Expenditures Paid by Government	Health Care Percent of GDP
Japan	83.0	2.4	2,878*	80.8*	8.5%
Spain	81.8	3.3	3,067	73.6	9.5%
Italy	81.8	3.7	3,137	77.9	9.5%
Australia	81.6	4.3	3,445*	68.0*	8.7%
UK	80.4	4.6	3,487	84.1	9.8%
France	81.0	3.9	3,978	77.9	11.8%
Germany	80.3	3.5	4,218	76.9	11.6%
US	78.0	6.5	7,960	47.7	17.4%

Source; OECD All statistics for 2009 except as noted - * indicates statistics for 2008

The sad part here is that the U.S. spends almost twice as much on health care per capita than the average and 47% more as a percentage of GDP than the next closest country, yet by measurements of life expectancy and infant mortality we perform the worst. As mentioned in Chapter 1, the U.S. will spend $735 billion on Medicare and Medicaid in 2011. If we closed just half the gap on per capita health care expenditures between us and Germany, the next closest in spending, that would be $1,871 per person or a 23.5% reduction. If that percentage applied to Medicare and Medicaid it would represent annual savings of $173 billion. If applied to our total population of 312 million people, a per capita savings of $1,871 would result in a total reduction in health care expenditures nationwide of $584 billion. Yes that's correct, $584 billion. Use of averages can be misleading because as they say, "the devil is in the details."

Wonder why U.S. healthcare is so expensive and why health insurance companies have to deny claims to make a decent profit? Consider this: in 2009 and 2010, Stephen Hemsley, CEO of United Health Group earned total compensation of $150 million for the two year period. So he averages about $37,000 per hour. That's not a typo. Sure that included stock and cash compensation but come on, it's still a cost the company has to make up in its profit. For that amount alone they could have provided health care for over 12,000 families for a full year. Still think public health care is without a doubt a bad idea? Think about the countries that provide better health care for *all* for less than the U.S. spends on health care for *some*. About 84% of our citizens currently have health insurance. Doesn't sound bad? That means over 50 million American have no health insurance.

What are we doing? How can we, the most advanced country in the world be so bad at managing our health care system? One fact may be that in every other country most health care is government provided. Many people claim that Medicare is a management disaster so why would we turn health care over to another government entity to screw it up more? The fact is that the health care companies are not doing us any great service by denying coverage and dropping people when they get sick after years of paying premiums.

The one fact that no one ever seems to point to when criticizing Medicare is that it is automatically selected against. Here is what that means. Insurance is a business designed around the concept of the law of averages, sometimes called the law of large numbers. The premise is that if you have enough subjects in your population, the results will revert to the average of the population. For example, we all buy fire insurance to protect us if our homes burn down. For the vast majority of us that will never happen. So 500 of us pay $500 each and when one house burns down the insurance company pays to replace it. But the insurer needs enough participants so that an average or expected number burns down. This assumes our population in total is average. If they wrote 500 policies on people who made homemade fireworks in their basement and smoked while doing it you would not expect an average number of fires. Similarly, Medicare insures the oldest members of our population who obviously need more hip replacements, cancer treatments and medications than the population in general. Of course Medicare is ridiculously expensive. However, the private health care system would never accept such a poor group of risks.

Some feel the problem is litigation, malpractice and the related insurance and claims costs. They claim this is causing doctors to do excessive procedures as a defensive measure. A survey was conducted by the Massachusetts Medical Society to determine the extent of these excessive procedures:

> Lead researchers were Manish K. Sethi, M.D., of the Department of Orthopedic Surgery of Massachusetts General Hospital and a member of the Medical Society's Board of Trustees and its Committee on Professional Liability, and Robert H. Aseltine, Jr., Ph.D., of the Institute for Public Health Research at the University of Connecticut Health Center in Farmington. "This survey clearly shows that the fear of medical liability is a serious burden on health care," said Dr. Sethi. "The fear of being sued is driving physicians to

defensive medicine and dramatically increasing health care costs. This poses a critical issue, as soaring costs are the biggest threat to the success of Massachusetts health reform efforts."

Physicians were asked about their use of seven tests and procedures: plain film X-rays, CT Scans, Magnetic Resonance Imaging (MRIs), ultrasounds, laboratory testing, specialty referrals and consultations, and hospital admissions. The results were self-reported by the physicians responding to the survey.

The results showed that 83 percent of the physicians surveyed reported practicing defensive medicine and that an average of 18 to 28 percent of tests, procedures, referrals and consultations and 13 percent of hospitalizations were ordered for defensive reasons.

The cost is in billions of dollars. Sethi and Aseltine estimated the costs of the tests to be $281 million for the eight specialties surveyed, based on Medicare reimbursements rates in Massachusetts for 2005-2006. In addition, the cost of unnecessary hospital admissions was estimated to be $1.1 billion, for a combined total estimate of nearly $1.4 billion. These numbers are for just one state.

Another argument for the excessive spending on health care is simply that doctors are paid on a fee for service basis. That is, they are paid for each procedure performed and are therefore incentivized to perform more tests and order more procedures. The U.S. is one of the few developed countries in the world without universal health care (i.e. health care for everyone.) Perhaps a brief look at France and Italy will tell us something about why we are doing it so wrong.

The World Health Organization ("WHO") performs numerous studies of the effectiveness and efficiency of health care worldwide. In a study last completed in 2000, they ranked overall health care delivery systems in 191 countries. This study ranked France #1, Italy #2 and the U.S. #37. As can be seen from the previous table, we spend almost twice as much as any other country on health care and have by far the highest infant mortality rate and the shortest life expectancy.

In ranking the health care systems of the world, WHO considered a number of factors in their studies:

The first is improvement in the health of the population (both in terms of levels attained and distribution). The second is enhanced responsiveness of the health system to the legitimate expectations of the population. Responsiveness in this context explicitly refers to the non-health improving dimensions of the interactions of the populace with the health system, and reflects respect of persons and client orientation in the delivery of health services, among other factors. As with health outcomes, both the level of responsiveness and its distribution are important. The third intrinsic goal is fairness in financing and financial risk protection. The aim is to ensure that poor households should not pay a higher share of their discretionary expenditure on health than richer households, and all households should be protected against catastrophic financial losses related to ill health.

France is a unique blend of private and public health care that offers choice yet in a regulated environment. In France, essentially everyone is covered through funding from payroll taxes paid mainly by employers. The tax to cover this is quite high, 12.8% paid by employers and 5.5% paid by employees (18.3% total). This might increase even further since the national health insurance program has been running a deficit for years. That sounds really high, but let's remembers that takes the place of health insurance payments by employers and employees in the U.S. which can run this high or higher. There are a myriad of health plans offered with prices varying widely from a few hundred dollars to several thousand. Assume for the sake of an example a family policy in the U.S. costs $750 per month (not an unrealistic assumption) and the employer pays half. That's a total cost of $9,000 per year. On an employee earning a salary of $50,000 per year that equates to 18% of salary. On an employee earning just $35,000 it equates to 25.7% of salary. Suddenly 18.3% doesn't sound so outrageous. Of course, in the U.S., the employer has the option to not offer health insurance, although under the new health care laws going into effect over the next several years they will now pay a fine for failure to do so.

Everyone in France has access to the same basic coverage. I guess their members of Parliament (Congress) have to live with what they hoist upon the rest of the population. Copayments are quite large ranging from 10% to 40%, which probably reduces unnecessary use of health care. The poor, who cannot afford these co pays, pay nothing. Because of these large copayments, many people have private complementary health insurance to cover the co pay. About 36% of France's doctors are public servants working in public hospitals and are essentially employees on salary. French doctors in private practice are paid by the national health insurance system based on a fee schedule, but doctors can charge a higher price and those who can afford to do so would go to that provider and pay the higher price if they believe that doctor is a higher quality health care provider. The patient or their private insurance must pay the difference between the fee charged by the doctor and the amount paid for by the universal health care system. The average French doctor earns about €40,000 ($58,000), although medical school is free and they don't have to deal with legal issues. Also, the French government pays two-thirds of the social security tax for most French physicians, a tax that's typically 40% of income.

On average 70 percent of the cost of a visit to a French family doctor or specialist is paid for. However, for more serious or chronic conditions, a much higher level of coverage is paid for by the national plan. For major surgery reimbursement can be 95 percent and for pregnancy and childbirth 95 to 100 percent. A patient can receive 100 percent coverage for chronic or acute medical conditions (including cancer, heart disease, etc.), requiring long-term care or a hospital stay of more than 30 days. These practices probably tend to discourage people from over utilizing medical care for minor issues. Something must be working because they spend about half as much per capita as the U.S., have a longer life expectancy and an infant mortality rate equal to 60% of that in the U.S. Sure they may have to wait an extra week or two for that MRI. So what. Unless your doctor just discovered a growth in your brain why should it matter? Perhaps we can no longer afford instantaneous responses to our health care needs in America.

Let's shift gears and focus on Italy, which was ranked as the world's second best health care system. My mother sure agrees. A few years ago she was in Italy when she tripped and fractured a bone in her foot. She ended up at an Italian hospital where they did x-rays and ended up putting a cast on her foot. The price was ridiculous.....ly low. They charged her nothing and sent her on her way. I don't think they even asked her name.

Italy also has a national health system that is comprised mainly of a public system along with some private insurance and facilities. Doctors who are part of the public system are paid a fixed fee for each patient and act as gatekeepers for other services. This is very much like the Health Maintenance Organization ("HMO") model in the U.S. They then refer patients to specialists as needed. Hospitals are paid on a fee for service basis based on the service provided and a set fee for each service. These plans offer less choice for the patient in terms of physician, specialist and hospital but are better at controlling cost. There is also frequently a long waiting period for certain services like mammograms, MRI's etc.

Routine care is free in Italy, but some diagnostic procedures and prescriptions carry co pays of up to 30%. However, 40% of the population (elderly, children, pregnant women) is exempt from these co pays.

About one third of Italians purchase some private health insurance. This allows them more freedom of physician and the use of private hospitals as opposed to public facilities. Private hospitals in Italy have excellent accommodations, some of which are comparable to five-star hotels. The comfort and the quality of service in private hospitals are superior but the medical care is similar to that of public hospitals. Private hospital treatments in Italy are much more expensive than public facilities.

The national health system is funded through payroll taxes imposed on employees and employers. The tax rather than growing at higher income levels starts at 10.6% of income then drops to 4.6% and then to zero at higher income levels. Everyone is paying their share regardless of income.

So why is the U.S. ranked 37th? The answer is likely in the detailed statistics. While the U.S. does provide some publicly funded health care such as Medicare, Medicaid, Veterans Health Administration programs we are the only developed nation without a national health insurance program covering substantially all citizens. Perhaps this, along with our lower life expectancy, leads to the low ranking. Is that lower life expectancy tied directly to health care or are there other drivers? The life expectancy in the U.S. varies and is higher for the more affluent who can afford health insurance and medical treatment.

In an article "Do Rich People Live Longer" in U.S. News Kimberly Palmer reported the following:

> Those looking for a magic elixir to keep them healthy and happy need look no further than their bank account. Wealth and, more broadly, socioeconomic status, play a powerful role in determining how long we live.

> "It's clear that those who have less wealth will have fewer years to live than those with more wealth," says James Smith, senior economist at the research group RAND. The connection is so widely accepted that researchers have given it a name: "the wealth gradient in mortality." What's far more complicated to understand is why the connection exists, and whether wealth causes better health, or vice versa.

> "Indeed," says Smith, "one hypothesis is that more-educated people are more forward-looking, and when they make decisions, they take into account the future more than uneducated people. A lot of things you might do, don't have an immediate negative impact— excessive drinking, smoking, and doing drugs can feel

good in the short-term - but the fact is it's going to kill you in the future." Another possibility is that people with higher levels of education are more likely to maintain their health, have better access to healthcare, and follow doctors' directions when it comes to taking pills or other instructions.

So in countries where the poor are provided with the benefit of health care it would seem logical that those people would have a longer life expectancy than poor people in America. While the other factors stated above play a role, clearly lack of access to health care for a large portion of the population due to economic status clearly will play a role in reducing overall life expectancy.

Most of these people get their coverage through their places of employment and because they are in group plans, they are not declined or rated at an unaffordable premium because of preexisting conditions.

You drastically reduce your risk of stroke and heart attack by preventive measures such as controlling cholesterol and blood pressure. If you can't afford routine health care, you go without such preventive measures until the worst happens. In essentially every other country, national health insurance programs provide all citizens with access to routine health care and treatment when needed.

In the U.S., people were protesting in the streets over health care reform. They don't want to pay for health care for everyone, just themselves. Let the lazy and unemployed go to hell. They should work hard too. Are they right or wrong? Do we believe that we should provide this basic human need to all of our citizens? Every other civilized nation does. Yes there are people who don't deserve it. They are lazy and unmotivated and want everything handed to them. But that is a small part of the population. The vast majority wants to work and would welcome the ability to provide for themselves and their families. They just can't either due to loss of jobs or inadequate education.

When someone lacks routine health care, they don't seek service until there is an emergency. When an uninsured person has a heart attack or stroke and is rushed to the hospital they are not thrown out on the street. They generally receive the care they need. Who pays for that care? You do, if you pay for health insurance, taxes, co pays... It is all built into the cost of our system. What might we save if that person were instead to take a daily pill to reduce blood pressure at a cost of $100 per month instead of needing $50,000+ in hospital care for a heart attack? Why might it be that we are the only country that protests so adamantly against making health care available for all? Could we all benefit in the end?

The reinvention of our multi-trillion dollar health care system would be an incredibly complex process. Our system is mainly comprised of private providers, doctors, hospitals, pharmacies and clinics. Reverting to a national and perhaps more public health care system as most of the rest of the world has done would be a gargantuan undertaking racked with resistance. But maybe it's time to rethink our system. Perhaps France and Italy can teach us something. A public system of care, without all of the legal entanglements, and access for all, might just be in our best interest. Private systems could then allow those able to afford it the opportunity to purchase better or more advanced treatments and utilize more luxurious accommodations for their health care needs. At some point we should realize our system is incredibly inefficient and consuming an ever growing piece of our pie.

CHAPTER IV

EDUCATION SYSTEM

Is Money the Problem?

The U.S. education system is among the poorest performing in the developed world. The literacy rates among fourth grade students in America are sobering. According to The National Center for Education Statistics, a part of the U.S. Department of Education, one out of three students scored "below basic" on the 2011 National Assessment of Education Progress Reading Test. A student is considered below basic if they cannot read an informative article and recognize the main purpose. About half of these low performing students come from low-income families. More than 67 percent of all US fourth graders scored "below proficient," meaning they are not reading at grade level. OECD reported that the U.S. placed 25th out of 30 countries in math performance and 21st in science performance. American students take an international test at age 15 with students from 40 countries and the Americans place 25th. Yet, in our budget issues, education is one of the areas experiencing the biggest budget cuts by state and municipal governments. We are perpetuating the poverty problem in America by poorly educating our children.

But wait, are budget cuts really the cause of the poor performance of our education system? Of the twenty nine countries included in the OECD study, the U.S. has one of the highest levels of education expenditure per capita of all countries. Our spending per student is 35% above the average and only Norway, Switzerland and Luxembourg spend more per student than the U.S. On primary education, our spending is double the average of all included countries. Only Israel and Iceland spend a larger percentage of GDP on education.

In his report 'Stupid in America', John Stossel reported the following:

> Ben Chavis is a former public school principal who now runs an alternative charter school in Oakland, Calif., that spends thousands of dollars less per student than the surrounding public schools. He laughs at the public schools' complaints about money.
>
> "That is the biggest lie in America. They waste money," he said.
>
> To save money, Chavis asks the students to do things like keep the grounds picked up and set up for their

own lunch. For gym class, his students often just run laps around the block. All of this means there's more money left over for teaching.

Even though he spends less money per student than the public schools do, Chavis pays his teachers more than what public school teachers earn. His school also thrives because the principal gets involved. Chavis shows up at every classroom and uses gimmicks like small cash payments for perfect attendance.

Since he took over four years ago, his school has gone from being among the worst in Oakland to being the best. His middle school has the highest test scores in the city.

If Not Money, Then What Drives Our Poor Performance?

If it isn't spending, which the data would seem to indicate, why is our education system in such poor shape?

Many experts propose several reasons:

1. Our schools are a government monopoly with no competition or incentive to improve. If you don't like the performance of your child's school, too bad. Unless you

are rich and can afford private schools, you have no choice.

2. Poor performing teachers are tolerated. There is no reward for top performers and we do not attract them. In countries with top performing schools, teachers are recruited from the top of their class. In business, good performing employees are rewarded with more money and opportunities. Poor performers are terminated, or at least paid less. In our public education system, thanks in part to teachers unions and government regulation, bad teachers face no such consequences and great teachers are not rewarded. Politicians refuse to change these conditions for fear of losing votes. Everyone wants to blame teachers, but it isn't all about the school.

3. Parents need to be involved and take an interest in their children's' education. There are 8,760 hours in a year. Children are in class generally 6 hours per day and 180 days per year or a total of 1,080 hours. So, children spend 12% of the year in the classroom. What's happening the other 88% of their time? Are parents making sure they do homework? Are they making sure their children even go to school? How can our schools do it all while controlling such a small percentage of students' time?

Don't think teaching methods and quality can make a difference? Here is another example from John Stossel's report.

> "I talked with 18-year-old Dorian Cain in South Carolina, who was still struggling to read a single sentence in a first-grade level book when I met him. Although his public schools had spent nearly $100,000 on him over 12 years, he still couldn't read.

> "So "20/20" sent Dorian to a private learning center, Sylvan, to see if teachers there could teach Dorian to read when the South Carolina public schools failed to.

> "Using computers and workbooks, Dorian's reading went up two grade levels -- after just 72 hours of instruction."

This example has nothing to do with money. It has to do with quality teaching.

Today in our system, there is no incentive to bring in quality teachers. That is not to say all teachers are bad. In fact, there are many excellent teachers in our education system. Unfortunately, when they come up with a better way of doing things, there is no avenue to share that information throughout our education system because there are some 15,000 school districts in the U.S. all acting independently and, in many cases, run by administrators and bureaucrats with no experience in education.

Where the U.S. is falling woefully behind, and an area that will limit our ability to innovate into the future, is in math and science. China and India dwarf the U.S. in graduates with degrees in math, science and engineering. In the coming years they will be the economic and innovation leaders. India produces 600,000 engineers per year compared to 84,000 produced by the U.S. For every 100,000 employees 25 to 34 years old in the workforce in U.S., 1,472 have degrees in math, science or engineering. In Korea that number is 3,555 and the OECD average for the thirty developed countries in its 2011 education study is 1,829. We are 20% below the average and only seven of the thirty countries ranked below the U.S. In addition, a 2008 National Science Foundation study found that in 2005, 59 percent of all doctoral degrees and 43 percent of all higher-education degrees in engineering and science in the U.S. were awarded to temporary residents. This basically means that a minority of the small number of advanced engineering and science degrees earned in the U.S. are earned by Americans. This accounts for the fact that U.S. businesses are hiring thousands of foreign engineers to work in their companies, especially technology driven companies. Drive through the heart of Silicon Valley in Northern California, the heart of technology innovation in America. Foreign workers abound. High tech companies are lobbying for more work visas for foreign workers because of the tremendous need for workers with science and engineering majors. These are some of the highest paying jobs in America yet an inadequate number of American students are qualified to accept these positions. Most come from countries that are eating America's lunch at educating their students. These people are filling some of the highest paying jobs available.

Few students who enter engineering majors at U.S. colleges are able to complete the curriculum. Only 36% of white students, and 20+% of black and Latino students in science, math and engineering programs were able to complete their degrees within five years. My oldest son earned an electrical engineering degree from Penn State. I remember him telling me that within only the first few weeks over half of his freshman physics class had dropped the class and were certainly headed out of the engineering program. Why is this happening? Certainly, the students coming out of our high schools are ill prepared for the rigors of advanced math and science curriculums.

Are the Poor at a Disadvantage?

Let's shift back to a discussion on the rich versus the poor, or, more appropriately, the educated vs. the non educated. According to a Newsweek report, by age three kids with professional parents are already a full year ahead of their poorer peers. They know twice as many words and score 40 points higher on IQ tests. By age 10, the gap is three years. By then, some poor children have not mastered basic reading and math skills, and many never will: this is the age at which failure starts to become irreversible.

Those of you who have had the benefits of birth should understand that your success may well have been ensured by virtue of your birth advantage in life. If you are born to educated or affluent parents you essentially are at a distinct advantage to those born into poor and uneducated families. This advantage also includes where you live. Certainly children in more affluent families live in better areas where we typically see better schools. Going to a gang infested school in an inner city slum cannot in any way foster the same learning environment as a school in an affluent suburb where most children are raised with the belief that an education is important and the parents of children who fall behind hire tutors to ensure their children keep up. Hence the birth advantage.

The World's Top Performing School System

So what works in the education field? It will probably surprise you if I tell you that Finland ranks number one in the world for its education system. This country is not one of the world powerhouses we think of when we talk about leading nations in any category. How are they different than the U.S. when it comes to education? Basically in every way possible.

In Finland, teaching is the most highly respected profession, above medical doctors. The best and brightest with advanced degrees voluntarily become teachers. Poor performing teachers don't last. In order to attract the best, teachers in Finland are well paid. An elementary school teacher makes $45-50/hour. A high school teacher makes $75-80/hour.

Remarkably, students and teachers in Finland spend significantly less time in school than American children. By age 15 Finnish students will have spent the equivalent of three years less schooling than U.S. students, yet they significantly outperform Americans at every level. And get this, they spend about one-third less per child on education than we do in the U.S. Why are we so bad at managing our schools? Let's look at how schools in Finland differ from schools in the U.S.

In their report <u>Finland: Slow and Steady Reform for Consistently High Results</u> the OECD offers a number of reasons, including the following:

1. The first thing to note is that these schools offer more than education. These are full-service schools. They provide a daily hot meal for every student. They provide health and dental services. They offer guidance and psychological counseling, and access to a broader array of mental health and other services for students and families in need. None of these services is means-tested. Their availability to all reflects a deep societal commitment to the well-being of all children.

2. Both regular class teachers (grades 1-6) and subject teachers (7-9) exercise an enormous degree of professional discretion and independence. While there is a national core curriculum in Finland, over the past 20 years it has become much less detailed and prescriptive. It functions more as a framework, leaving education providers and teachers latitude to decide what they will teach and how. Teachers select their own textbooks and other instructional materials, for example. With the professional autonomy Finnish teachers enjoy comes very substantial responsibility for tasks that in other systems are typically handled more

centrally. Chief among these are curriculum and assessment. The national core curriculum is really a framework rather than a roadmap, leaving teachers an enormous amount of discretion to interpret that framework, select their own textbooks and other curriculum materials, and then design their own lessons, all of which require time. In some schools the process of curriculum development is undertaken collaboratively by teams of teachers, while in smaller schools the responsibility might fall largely on each individual teacher.

3. The quality of teachers and teaching lies at the heart of Finland's educational success. Teaching has long been a respected occupation in Finland, but until the teacher education reform act of 1979, there was little sense that teachers required much advanced training. After completing upper secondary school, prospective primary and secondary teachers enrolled in a seminarium (teacher college) for two or three years of mostly practical training and then moved straight into the classroom.

4. Furthermore, it is not left solely to the discretion of the regular class teacher to identify a problem and alert the special teacher. Every comprehensive school has a

"pupils' multi-professional care group," as described by Riitta Aaltio, principal of a 360-student primary school in Kerava, just outside Helsinki. The group meets at least twice a month for two hours. The group consists of the principal, the special education teacher, the school nurse, the school psychologist, a social worker, and the teachers whose students are being discussed. The parents of any child being discussed are contacted prior to the meeting and are sometimes asked to be present. Principal Aaltio describes the group's function as follows: In each meeting we usually have enough time to discuss two classes of pupils with their class (i.e. homeroom) teacher, plus any "acute cases." First, we talk about the class and how things are going in general. If there are any concerns – learning, teaching, social climate – or some problems with individual students we try to decide what kind of support we can provide. If we believe a pupil needs professional help beyond what we can provide at the school, we help the family get that kind of help be it medical, psychological, or social.

5. Because Finnish teachers are highly educated and are accustomed to being in full control of their own classroom, they have no tradition of principals actively visiting classes to monitor the quality of teaching in their

schools. In fact, given the small school sizes, most principals are themselves teaching at least a few hours a week, so their role is a mixed one.

Finnish teachers generally all possess master's degrees and come from the top third of their class and are allowed to utilize their talents somewhat freely. U.S. teachers are not allowed the freedom to utilize their talents nor do we compensate them in a way top students would demand. Teachers with degrees in math and science, disciplines with more demand for skilled teachers due to the complexity of the material, are hard to attract because they are also in demand in business and can earn much higher salaries. Because of government bureaucracy and union rules, we can't pay a sufficient additional amount for a teacher with a master's degree in math than we can for one who teaches social studies.

Really this distinction between U.S. and Finnish schools boils down to a few key points: highly competent and educated teachers, freedom for competent teachers to do their jobs, cooperation among teachers and administrators to solve pupils' issues and administrators who are also educators. Note that additional budget or spending is not one of the points mentioned. Between the politicians and the teachers unions, we would never be able to operate our schools in such a manner in the U.S. Our leaders have saddled us with one of the most expensive, yet poorest performing school systems in the entire developed world. Don't blame the politicians who want to cut spending. Spending is not the problem in our schools, competence is.

Why Not in America?

Could some of these lessons work in the U.S.? Is there any example in the U.S. of schools run locally with the educators in charge and politics and unions out of the picture? I earlier provided an example of how a charter school in Oakland, CA was significantly outperforming other public schools. Let's look at another alternative, Catholic schools. Private schools are not subject to as many state and federal regulations as public schools. They are not subject to the limitations of state education budgets and have more freedom in designing curriculum and instruction. Sound a little more like Finland?

Derek Neal, associate professor of economics at the University of Chicago conducted a study of the performance of Catholic Schools. He stated the following:

"...Catholic schools succeed in communities where public schools fail miserably. Ninety-one percent of blacks and Hispanics who attend Catholic secondary schools in urban counties graduate from high school. This figure does not include General Equivalence Diplomas (GED). In contrast, only sixty two percent of blacks and Hispanics who attend urban public schools graduate.

"However, critics of Catholic schools are quick to argue that Catholic as well as other private schools do not educate a random sample of students, that Catholic school students are, on average, from better educated and more stable families than public-school students. Therefore, high graduation rates in Catholic schools may rise because Catholic schools select good students, not because Catholic schools offer a better education.

"To address this issue, I constructed a statistical model of the determinants of high-school graduation. The results are striking. Consider a representative minority student in an urban public school. The student is representative in the following sense: Based on his observed characteristics, his predicted probability of graduating equals the overall graduation rate for urban minorities in public schools, 62 percent. Now consider an urban, Catholic school student with the same observed characteristics (namely, parent's education, parent's occupation, family structure, and reading materials at home). The predicted graduation rate for this student is 88 percent. "

Our school administrators, for some reason, fear attempts to improve. It seems like a case of self preservation or an unwillingness to even consider that someone else may be able to do it better than they can. They prefer to blame teachers, most of whom have no control over what or how they teach. Consider this:

Cardinal John J. O'Connor has repeatedly made New York City the following extraordinary offer: send me the lowest performing five percent of children presently in the public schools, and I will put them in Catholic schools—where they will succeed. Last August, the Cardinal sweetened the offer. He invited city officials to come study the Catholic school system, "to make available to public schools whatever of worth in our Catholic schools is constitutionally usable. The doors are open. Our books are open. Our hearts are open. No charge." The city's response: almost total silence. In a more rational world, city officials would have jumped at the Cardinal's offer. It might, first of all, have been a huge financial plus for the city. The annual per-pupil cost of Catholic elementary schools is $2,500 per year, about a third of what taxpayers now spend for the city's public schools.

Can the school officials in New York be any more ignorant? Why wouldn't you go see what the Cardinal has to offer? What do you have to lose? These are the people responsible for educating our leaders of tomorrow. Like an ostrich they bury their heads in the sand, ignore the problems and refuse to see the possibilities. This is a prime example of the problem with our schools nationwide. Is it any wonder our education system is ranked 25th when compared with other nations in the developed world?

So we all tolerate the situation and the U.S. is falling woefully behind the rest of the world despite one of the highest levels of spending in the world. So it seems money is not the issue. Perhaps with competent management and teaching we could spend even less on education and still provide a highly superior education to the one we provide today.

In 2007-2008 the U.S. spent approximately $506 billion on public school education. If our spending was in line with the OECD member country average, our expenditures would be reduced by $150 billion.

CHAPTER V

BIG BUSINESS

Why would corporations be included in a book about what is wrong with our government and our country in general? Three reasons:

1. They control a great deal of the wealth in America and "buy" congressional favors that benefit them every day.

2. While representing only a small percentage, some of our most prominent corporations have shown that they cannot be trusted. They are too often driven by total greed, even when it is to the detriment of our nation. While some greed may in fact be the driving force that made America the greatest economic engine in the history of the world, excessive greed has caused massive detrimental effects on our economy and our citizens.

3. Unfortunately, some of the largest and most profitable companies are led by unethical, inconsiderate and dishonest people who place themselves in higher regard than they do others. This leads many to assume that all successful companies and in fact successful

people are unethical and driven solely by insatiable greed, which is far from the truth.

With that said, let's pick on big business - they are just like the wealthy, so what the heck. Well, in fact, they and the wealthy are one in the same. Over 80% of corporate stocks are held by the richest 1% of Americans. Anything that benefits big business also benefits the 1%. They pay low taxes, control most of the wealth, and effectively own our government. To some they are just "those rotten greedy bastards." The government should just take all their money and shut them down. Who needs them? Oh wait, big business led America to be the most advanced country in the world and created tens of millions of jobs. Uh, oh, did these people speak too soon?

If you outright hate big business just because they make a lot of money, think again. Many people hear a company made billions of dollars and curse them for being greedy. They forget how big these companies are and how much shareholder money is invested. We need big corporations. Without them I wouldn't be writing this on a computer, we wouldn't have airplanes, affordable automobiles, inexpensive housing, movies, and life saving drugs or even our beloved cell phones. Our food and clothing would cost multiples of what it does today. But that wouldn't matter because many of us wouldn't have jobs so we couldn't buy those items anyway.

So why do we hate these companies so much? Well, I'll tell you why. Even though we have the second highest nominal corporate tax rates in the world, without a doubt many of the largest most profitable corporations do not pay their fair share. As discussed in Chapter II, companies making tens of billions in profits pay a lower tax rate than many individuals. The myriad of tax credits and exclusions they bribed (yes that is certainly the correct verb usage) our legislators into passing allow them to drastically reduce their actual tax rates.

Yes, big business helped build our once strong middle class. Our ancestors earned good wages producing high quality automobiles, appliances, steel, recreational items and even clothing. These people worked tirelessly to produce those items, and then took the good wages they earned and spent them on the very products they produced. This drove our economic engine. The purchase of these goods drove American companies to new heights. They were, in effect, producing their own customers. And those customers drove the need for companies to produce more goods and therefore employ their new customers. The circle was complete. Can you say "trickle-up economics?"

Somewhere along the line, the chain was broken. Big business continues to want to sell their product to their customers but the customers are disappearing. They are finding their customers in China and India, not in America. In an effort to reduce costs, they moved production facilities to countries with much lower wage bases, in many cases sacrificing the quality and even safety of their products. They could now produce these items at a much lower cost. There are two problems with this strategy:

1. They have lost many of their customers in America. The once proud hard working middle class is moving en mass into poverty, or at best lower class. People who once made a good living producing the products that made America strong now work for minimum wage and no benefits at the two largest employers in America – Wal-Mart and McDonalds. We are becoming a country of "haves" and "have nots." Unfortunately, the haves are becoming a smaller group but with more money and the have nots are growing in leaps and bounds. Once hard working people with good jobs and successful businesses are now sleeping in cars or on relatives' couches. Most of the wealth growth in America is going to a shrinking minority. Today, a record 40 million Americans are on food stamps. Based on our current trend, America will become an impoverished nation with massive slums filled with chronically uneducated and unemployed people with no hope and no path to prosperity.

2. The second problem with corporate moves to other countries is one for America, not for the companies. When they move jobs overseas they also move entities and profits so they no longer pay taxes in the U.S. on the profits made in those operations. So now we have large numbers of unemployed, who obviously don't pay taxes and big American businesses making their profits in foreign subsidiaries, and therefore paying no U.S. taxes on those earnings. The circle is once again complete, only now it spells deficit, a deficit spiraling out of control. If this trend continues, America will spiral downward and will no longer be the market of choice for companies wishing to sell their goods.

For a larger and larger percentage of our population, America is crumbling from within. Perhaps no one cares now, but at some future point, America will be what India and China are to their poorest citizens. Our cities will become slums. Many of our citizens will be malnourished and sleeping in the streets. Declare me crazy, but the trends confirm the path we are on.

On November 27, 2011 Scott Pelley presented a report on 60 Minutes entitled, "Hard Times Generation," about the number of families and children in central Florida living in cars and the dangers and difficulties they face. One of the families profiled were the Metzgers. Arielle, 15 Austin, 13 and their father live in a van. They clean up in gas station rest rooms before school. They eat cold food out of cans. They live in constant fear during the night when they park their van and try to sleep. Their father, a carpenter has been out of work for several years. These are not lazy people who don't want to work. They used to be a middle class family, now they live in a car. Imagine yourself in that situation. Living comfortably in your nice home one day and losing absolutely everything the next. The next time you sit down to dinner with your family, or hop into a nice soft bed on a cold night and snuggle in with the covers pulled up to your neck, think about what it would be like to suddenly lose that and be spending the night in your car, worrying if the criminals on the street will prey on you during the night and take the few dollars you have left. Or worse yet, beat or rape you.

If you watched that report without a tear in your eye, something would have to be wrong with you. Too many people think that those who can't get along and need help are freeloaders and efforts to help them are just taking from the rich. It could happen to any of us. Many Americans are one serious illness or one accident or plant closure away from life in a car.

Today 45% of Americans, many with jobs do not earn enough to cover the basics of food, clothing, shelter and medical care.

Making matters worse, these people have no means to send their children to college so that they can better themselves.

Over 40 million Americans are now receiving food stamps. One in five children lives in poverty. Does anyone really believe that most of these people want to be in that situation? Does anyone really believe that they are too lazy to work and just want handouts? They are competing for jobs against foreign workers who earn less than $1.00 per hour. Is this the future of a large part of our middle class? Are their jobs gone to other countries forever? Once the middle class disappears, as it currently is, it will be nearly impossible to get it back. We will have the rich 10% or 20%, and the poor 80% or 90%.

Let's compare this group to the rich. More power to them. Unfortunately, this class is responsible for some of the most heinous crimes in America today. While committed by only a small percentage of the leaders of large corporations, their crimes are the most far reaching in terms of victims affected by them. Just one person's greed at this level can touch thousands or even millions of victims. CEO's and CFO's unsatisfied with their measly $5 million or $10 million per year pay packages are committing massive frauds that are destroying the lives of millions of people all in the name of insatiable greed. They are the companies we have all heard of, MCI/WorldCom, Enron, TYCO, America's largest banks and mortgage companies and the list could go on. Corporate titans committing fraud to jack up stock prices for their own personal gain beyond the tens of millions they are already earning. And throw the worst of them all, Bernie Madoff in with them.

And let's not forget the bankers on Wall Street. These are the people who made billions of dollars in profits by bundling toxic mortgages destined to default into supposedly low-risk, AAA rated securities that sent the housing market into a downward spiral and kicked off the great recession. This enabled people who were innately unqualified to buy homes they could not afford and even do so with no down payment. Home values skyrocketed and we all know what came next. An entire economy was brought to its knees and remains there today, five years later. And here is the icing on the cake. You, the American taxpayer, bailed these firms out when your tax dollars were used to bail out AIG who had written credit default swaps and sold them to these firms as protection. A credit default swap is essentially insurance for the lender in the event debt is not paid back. If a loan defaults the issuer of the swap steps in and pays the debt. AIG wrote billions of dollars in these swaps assuming they would never have to pay off. When the housing market collapsed and people were defaulting on mortgages AIG could not afford to make good on its promise to pay. Goldman Sachs had $20 billion in credit default swaps with AIG. Goldman Sachs had collected $7.5 billion from its AIG credit-default swaps but had an additional $13 billion at risk. As the market collapsed, the U.S. Government bailed out AIG and Goldman collected on their swaps as did many other banks including many foreign institutions. In any event, all of these firms were bailed out with your tax dollars. Of course, the alternative of letting a number of banks become insolvent would have been catastrophic for the worldwide economy, which was already on shaky ground.

So, people who lost their jobs and are on food stamps today helped to bail out the firms whose leaders earn $10 million or $20 million per year and complain about paying more taxes.

So if everyone resents what off shoring is doing to our nation, why are these companies moving our jobs to other countries? The explanation is quite simple. Every day, you and I are telling them to do it. We want to go to Target or Wal-Mart and buy that polo shirt for $7.99 or that coffee maker for only $12.99. We reinforce this behavior every time we pull out our wallets. Individually we can do nothing about it, but together we can reverse this trend simply by buying American made products. We curse big business for exporting jobs then, support and even encourage their behavior as we seek out and purchase low-cost, foreign-produced goods.

We can't buy everything, made in America, simply because some products are not available from American companies. We also need active international trade because many jobs in America are the result of products we export. Unfortunately, the trade gap is simply too out of balance. As just one example of the imbalance, in September of 2011, the U.S. had a trade imbalance (the difference between the value of goods and services we export versus the amount we import) of $43 billion. That means we imported $43 billion more in goods than we exported, resulting in a net outflow of money to other countries. Of that, $29 billion went to China. Annualized, that represents a $350 billion deficit with China annually. That means $350 billion American dollars flowed into China. Is it any wonder the U.S. Government owes China over $1 trillion? Remember, $1 trillion is $1,000 billion.

Why is China responsible for such a large portion of our trade deficit? We have all heard about the low wages people in China earn. Obviously, if you can pay your factory workers $1.00 per hour, or even much less than that, it makes the goods very cheap to produce.

In addition, many feel the Chinese government keeps its currency undervalued and does not allow it to float freely in relation to other worldwide currencies. This makes their products even cheaper. Here's why. Let's suppose in a free market, the Chinese Yuan should be worth $1.00 U.S. The Chinese government, with its giant trade surplus, buys dollars and floods the market with Yuan, driving its value down. So now the Yuan is worth only $.75. So when they pay a factory worker one Yuan to produce a product, the cost should be $1.00 U.S. but now it is only $.75 U.S.

In addition to devaluing their currency, the Chinese government subsidizes many of its industries, making them an unfair competitor. So as one example China's steel production has more than doubled since 2003, while U.S. production has dropped by nearly 40 percent. According to a report by the Economic Policy Institute titled, "Unfair China Trade Costs Local Jobs," the U.S.'s trade imbalance with China cost the U.S. 2.4 million jobs between 2001 and 2008. The Chinese government also allows its companies to produce counterfeit American goods. So when Callaway Golf comes out with a hot new driver, China is shipping knock offs within a matter of weeks, stealing American jobs and cheating the buyers who think they are getting the real deal, but instead are receiving an inferior product. Why doesn't Congress take action against China? Why not tax Chinese goods imported to America? Because the current system results in high returns on U.S. investments in China, making the rich richer while it reduces the value of American labor and eliminates job opportunities.

So the more money we send to other countries, the less money there is in America for Americans. Of course, the U.S. won't run out of money, we will just print more. As we discussed earlier, the more we print, the less each dollar is worth. Therefore, as we print more, we have to spend an ever increasing amount to purchase products from other countries. It's a constant cycle, just like the companies who are, in effect, eliminating their customers by outsourcing their jobs overseas. Oh, they will continue to have plenty of customers, just not in the United States. Somehow, somewhere we will need to break the cycle, or the downward spiral of America will continue.

So where is all of this leading? U.S. News reported that we are now in a situation where one in every two Americans are considered poor or low income. Fifty percent are poor in what we continue to think is the greatest nation on earth. Well, for half of our citizens it is anything but the greatest nation on earth.

"Safety net programs such as food stamps and tax credits kept poverty from rising even higher in 2010, but for many low-income families with work-related and medical expenses, they are considered too 'rich' to qualify," said Sheldon Danziger, a University of Michigan public policy professor who specializes in poverty. "The reality is that prospects for the poor and the near poor are dismal," he said. "If Congress and the states make further cuts, we can expect the number of poor and low-income families to rise for the next several years."

Most of these people want to work. Many are working but their jobs just don't pay enough. Some say too bad, they have no skills. Well, their children will also grow up with no opportunities. Not because they are lazy but because in the name of higher profit, the jobs that supported what Tom Brokaw called, The Greatest Generation, are gone, probably for good. To make matters worse for these people, the longer they are unemployed, the harder it is to find another job. How will these people ever pull out of this dismal situation? Where will the good paying jobs come from in the future?

I have seen job ads saying, "long term unemployed need not apply." What kind of person would do that? What kind of company would allow it? I can only hope these people get a chance to experience what the people they are excluding are suffering through. Perhaps if they lost their jobs and health coverage, and then experienced a serious health issue, they might realize what absolutely miserable, inconsiderate people they are.

What do we see happening in foreign countries where poverty is rampant? Desperate people living in slums without the basic needs. Drug cartels. Kidnappings for ransom. Beggars in the streets. It absolutely can, and is happening here. Is this what we see as the future of America? We see the "Occupy Protests" happening throughout the country. This is a sure sign that many are not just dissatisfied, but see no future. No hope. Is this what we want? America is so focused on greed and protecting the wealthy few that we don't even see it. We think "make the rich richer and they will hire everyone and give them high paying jobs." It isn't going to happen. Think back to the example in Chapter II, Part II, and my example of the employer. Does the business hire more people because they are rich, because their taxes are lower or because there is more demand for their product? Do you believe the people sleeping in cars are going to buy their products and lead to a hiring spree? Trickle up economics is what made America a great nation. Sorry, President Reagan, trickle-down economics is a fallacy. It just doesn't work.

We have become so caught up in excessive greed that we now confuse it with success. It will be the undoing of America as the world leader. We have already fallen from our perch and are destroying our own. Our dollar is weak and buys less foreign goods than it once did.

So our big business family, who once created many of our good paying jobs and led us to prosperity, have negotiated their tax rates to practically nothing, and in some cases less than nothing, moved our best jobs overseas and committed catastrophic frauds upon the American people.

So are those all of the facts? Not exactly. In the interest of stating both sides, let's consider this from the point of view of the businesses. Corporations are entities formed by the investment of individuals' funds into a business. I think we all know that. What many do not understand is that corporations have but one mission. Their sole purpose is simply to maximize shareholder value. Shouldn't they be allowed to do anything within the law to accomplish that? Are they not violating their fiduciary duty if they do not strive to accomplish that mission? Management is entrusted with a fiduciary duty to use those funds in a profitable and responsible manner.

Somewhere along the line, we lost sight of that and began to believe that corporations were social entities, charged with operating solely for the common good. Companies in the U.S. are choking on excessive rules and regulations that are costing them billions in profits. These rules alone are enough to make a company want to move to another country. We hear about a company making billions in profits and people get all up in arms. To a massive corporation with hundreds of billions of dollars in shareholder wealth invested, a few billion of profit may actually represent a poor return on the investment of the shareholders. Return on equity (income divided by shareholder equity) is a more rational measure. A large multinational corporation with $300 billion in shareholder funds that earns $10 billion in profit is really only generating less than a 3.5% return for their investors. Who wants to invest their money to make 3.5%?

While the MCI's and Enron's of the world shake our confidence, they actually represent a very small minority. Most businesses are run in a responsible and ethical manner. Not working hard to maximize returns to investors would be the irresponsible thing.

Our liberal friends in Washington and many of their followers somehow got the idea that business is responsible for solving the problems of America that the Government has neglected to solve. Perhaps the biggest is health care. Businesses offered health care benefits to employees as a fringe benefit, additional compensation and an incentive to remain with the company. Now the Democrats want to force business to offer health care to employees, sometimes at great cost to the company. (Actually their first preference is to take health care out of the workplace and provide public health care.) Why? It isn't their responsibility. As we discussed in Chapter III, other developed nations provide health care for all of their citizens. The irony is they provide better health care at a lower cost than we do. Unlike the U.S. Government, they don't tell private enterprise "we can't figure it out so we are going to force you to."

Not all businesses are international, nor can they all relocate overseas to reduce costs. The statutory corporate tax rates in the U.S. are one of the highest in the world. So the big international corporation can move operations overseas to reduce its tax rate or lobby for special tax credits that benefit them alone but the small and midsized companies in the U.S. do not have this luxury and are saddled with higher rates. How can our companies export goods and compete internationally or even just in the U.S. if their operating costs and taxes are higher than their international competitors. It's a global world and we need to compete on all fronts. If our costs are much higher, our goods are unattractive as exports, so we will never reduce the trade deficit. If companies can't sell their products to other countries, many will have to eliminate jobs. Ah! The customer cycle works both ways.

Should we mandate that they produce their products in the U.S.? Not only would it not work, but it would be illegal. They would simply move their entire company to another county. Only you and I together can force change, by voting with our wallets. We all know it but no one does it. It's like a party. No one wants to be first to dig into the buffet. Why should I go buy the $15 American made shirt if you are going to go buy the $9 one at Wal-Mart? We hear it all the time. If we all just bought one item made in America we would create a certain number of jobs. The fact is American made products are also frequently better or at least safer.

Look at some of the great cheap products we imported from China. Drywall that made people sick and caused them to have to rip their homes apart to remove it. Dog food that killed over 100 pets and made hundreds sick. Let's keep those cheap products coming.

If we don't reverse the current trend, many in our middle class will find themselves in poverty in the coming years and decades.

CHAPTER VI

FIXING AMERICA

What would I do to fix America?

Federal Government:

The problem with our Government is that it is not of the people, by the people or for the people.   Especially our Congress, which is mired in partisan politics, and unable to solve any of the problems facing our country.   Votes on important issues fall too much by party lines. The members of our Government are bought and paid for, not always directly, but ultimately, they are pawns to special interests. While they tell a story during campaigns about their concern for all, they are ultimately totally indebted to the big business and wealthy individuals who contribute large amounts to their campaigns. They make poor decisions that cost our country billions for reasons we can all just wonder about.

In no uncertain terms, the management of the United States is incompetent.   We spend more than almost every other developed nation on health care and education, yet we rank near the bottom in both categories. We, the leaders of the free world, recently had our government on the verge of financial collapse because the imbeciles making our laws couldn't work together on a compromise.

Our elected officials need to be focused on what is best for all of America, not just the few. Why should Congress be held hostage by big business and millionaires and their friends? Not that we should ignore what is best for the wealthy - they are citizens too. In order to get America on sound financial footing, we need to raise taxes and cut spending. The Republicans refuse to raise taxes, even on the wealthiest Americans. The democrats refuse to cut spending. Something must give, or our national debt will just continue to soar out of control. Unfortunately, many citizens are screaming for cuts in spending without any idea of where the U.S. Government spends most of its funds.

Some Republicans who are fortunately no longer running for President are proposing a flat tax or the most ridiculous of all, Herman Cain's 9-9-9 plan. That plan would be a millionaire's delight and further decimate our dying middle class. In fact, it would drastically increase taxes on people who can't even put food on their table or a roof over their heads. I can only say thank God, or thank the voters that guy dropped out of the race. All of these plans would further cut taxes on the wealthy and increase taxes on the poorest of our citizens. They almost universally eliminate capital gains taxes, a windfall that would further benefit only the wealthiest Americans.

We must cut spending, but it should not include Social Security, Medicare, Unemployment, Food Stamps or Housing Assistance. Social Security is not the government's money. It belongs to the people who contributed to it for decades. Many people depend almost entirely on Social Security for their basic survival. Why should we now punish them and make their lives miserable because our Government is inept?

Medicare is the only health care alternative for the elderly. Without it, they will not have access to health care. Ideas to give the elderly vouchers will leave them with nothing because the health insurers in America today will deny them coverage or price them out of the market. Think back to my example of how difficult it was for a generally healthy and responsible person like me to obtain health insurance. What would these companies do to an elderly person with an artificial hip and a history of cancer? Do you really want to throw your grandmother out on the street when she gets sick?

Unemployment, food stamps and housing assistance fill the most basic needs of our most needy citizens. Without them, millions more would be homeless and starving on the streets.

What we really need is a Congress elected based on their views and beliefs and not beholden to anyone. Under our current system it takes millions of dollars to get elected and the people who contribute that money will always have influence greater than their numbers. Campaign financing reform has been talked about many times but perhaps it is time for a more radical change in our electoral system. I would like to see reform whereby the U.S. Government pays the campaign costs for candidates. That may sound crazy on the surface but we need a radical change in America if this country has any chance of turning around its deteriorating position. I am not, by any means the first to propose public campaign financing. But there has not been enough grassroots support to get it done. It's time we stopped letting money buy our elected officials. I propose that anyone wishing to run for Congress be required to get a specified number of endorsement signatures. The number would be based on the size of their constituency. If they accomplish that, they would be allocated a fixed amount of campaign funds. Only the candidate with the most signatures from each party would qualify. If an independent candidate met the requirements, they would also qualify for funding. The amount of funding would also be based on the size of the constituency they need to reach out to. While this may sound like more government spending it would equate to a minuscule piece of our federal budget. Perhaps then we would have candidates elected based on their views and capabilities, not on how many rich friends they have. They would not have to do favors for special interests just so they could be assured of ongoing contributions for the next election.

That may sound like a lot of additional government spending but let's look at it. Suppose each candidate for senate received $7.5 million and there are three candidates in every race. That would total $22 million per election ($7.5 million x 3) but they only run every six years so the average would be $383 million per year ($22 million x 17 contests per year). Candidates for the House of Representatives cover a smaller area so assume we gave each $2 million. With three candidates in every race that would equate to a total of $2.6 billion. Since their terms are two years that would average $1.3 billion per year. So the annual average would be about $1.7 billion per year. Based on our current federal government spending, that would equal the amount the U.S. Government spends in a little over ten hours. It's less than we are spending to make and store presidential coins. In exchange we would get representatives in Congress who are not indebted to people who gave them large contributions. Instead they would answer only to the voters. And by the way, they wouldn't have to spend a large part of their time in office raising money for the next election; instead they could focus all of their attention on doing their job. Wouldn't that be a novel idea?

Sounds great to me. One problem. It can't happen. Why? There is a little thing called soft money. Hard money is money contributed directly to candidates and there are limits on how much individuals and businesses can contribute. This money can be used by the candidate to say, vote for me. Soft money is money given to the political parties or Political Action Committees ("PAC") and is totally unregulated as to amount. Soft money can be used to educate the public about issues, but can't say who to vote for. However, it can effectively be used to say who not to vote for. Here's an example.

> Candidate John runs an ad that says, "Candidate Bob is a bad person who wants to tax food stamps. Vote for me on election day." Because it says "Vote for me", this is a political ad, which must be paid for with hard money.

> Candidate John runs an ad that says, "Candidate Bob is a bad person who wants to tax food stamps. Be sure to vote on Election Day." Because the ad "educates" people on an issue and doesn't tell them to vote for John, it can be paid for by soft money. This type of ad would likely be run by a PAC, and that organization is

probably run by someone close to the candidate, and is likely to end up with a sweet job if the candidate gets elected. From a practical standpoint this is telling people to vote for John but it eliminates limits on spending. So a candidate with a major party can, from a practical standpoint spend a lot more campaigning for office than any limits we would put on them with a government paid campaign fund.

Candidates are theoretically separate from these PAC's. The truth is they are not anywhere near separate. Super PACs may raise unlimited sums of money from corporations, unions, associations and individuals and then spend unlimited sums to overtly advocate for or against political candidates. While Romney's SuperPAC, "Restore our Future" is not affiliated with the Romney campaign, an analysis by ABC News in August found that it is funded by many of the same people who have contributed to Romney. It is also staffed by several of Romney's former staffers. It has raised $43 million and $39 million has been spent to campaign against other republicans in the primaries to date.

Of the 90 donations to the PAC, approximately 57 came from Romney donors. Paul Edgerly, who works at Romney's former company, Bain Capital, donated the maximum $2,500 to the actual Romney campaign. However, he gave $500,000 to the SuperPAC. What's more, his wife Sandra did exactly the same thing.

Perhaps we could decide you can't spend soft money mentioning any candidates. There are likely nine men and women in long black robes who would say that violates a little thing called freedom of speech. This would perhaps require major federal legislation. That would only happen with overwhelming public support which would need to include massive election turnouts and a willingness to vote out the congressional incumbents who do not support the wishes of the public. Today, we vote like robots along party lines without knowing the real issues. Most people are too uninterested, apathetic or too busy to find out the facts and how their representatives voted on issues.

But we the voters also need to take responsibility for the stupid government. About 55% of voting age persons in America voted in the 2008 federal elections. In non Presidential election years, the turnout is generally less than 40%. Perhaps part of the reason is voter apathy because no one represents their views. Perhaps if candidates were selected based on broad appeal instead of fund raising ability the turnout would increase.

If we all don't get involved, we have no one to blame but ourselves for the total mismanagement of our nation. Look in the mirror. Chances are you are part of the problem. In addition to voting, voters need to let their representatives know what they think of their job performance while in office. We need to call them. Send letters and emails. Most importantly, we need to mobilize and vote them out of office when they do a poor job. Voter apathy will get us nowhere. The "occupy" protests are the beginning of a movement to tell Washington what at least some of their voters think.

Personal Income Taxes

Let me start by repeating my strong belief that trickledown economics does not work. It is trickle-up economics that built America. The personal income tax system is designed to allow the rich to accumulate more. Yes, they pay a lot more than the poor but that's because the poor and even middle class have little or nothing to pay with.

Luxury chain Neiman Marcus said in December 2011, it has sold out of the ten 2012 Ferrari sports cars it offered in its Christmas book of fantasy gifts for $395,000 each. No doubt sold to people who couldn't possibly afford to pay another 3% in taxes. As mentioned in Chapter II, when you look at taxes paid as a percentage of GDP the U.S. has one of the lowest tax burdens in the developed world. Why is it then that our citizens can't possibly afford to pay any more? Some wealthy people are stepping up and saying "tax me more, I can afford it." But certainly, they are the exception. Should we feel bad for the spoiled brats who have wealth given to them by mommy and daddy?

The arrogance and stupidity of some of these people is astounding. Take the case of John Fleming, a U.S. Congressman from Louisiana. He complained that he could not afford any more taxes. He owns businesses that gross $6.3 million of revenue and reportedly make a profit of about $600,000. He appeared on MSNBC and stated he can't afford any more taxes because after feeding his family he only has about $400,000 left. Apparently he wants us to believe he invests all of that back in his business and then has to hire more employees. Hogwash. Let me see his financial statements. In any event, he apparently has to feed his family on the meager $200,000 he takes out of the business. Oh, I guess he forgot to mention that he also gets $174,000 per year from his seat in Congress and a pretty nice package of benefits you and I would love to have. This guy is actually helping to run our country. How out of touch can any one person be without living on the moon?

The tax issues are not confined to the rich. The poorest of our citizens are stealing from the American taxpayer and being rewarded with thousands of dollars to thank them for being totally irresponsible and in some cases just downright lazy. They even have the nerve to complain when someone like me asks them if their claims to these benefits are legitimate. The fact is, however, no matter how much we try to tax them they have nothing to give.

Then there are the people with nice cash based businesses who live in nice homes, drive expensive cars, go on great vacations but don't make any money in their businesses. I wonder how that works. Of course that's no secret.

So what should we do? Here are my thoughts:

a. The Rich - Raise the rates a few percent for high incomes over $250,000, more on the super wealthy. Reverse the Bush tax cuts. I can't believe the outcry when Obama proposed this. They are 3% of the population. Don't let them kid anyone; their lives won't change one iota and they will still spend on the luxuries of life. The very wealthy spend little of their total income. Most is going into their investment portfolios which obviously continue to grow.

In addition there appears to be no correlation between tax rates and employment. In 1965 the top tax rate was 70% and unemployment was 4.5%. In 1980 the top tax rate was 70% and unemployment was 7.1%. In 2010 the top tax rate was 35% and unemployment was 9.6%. Since 1980, the top tax rate on ordinary income has been cut in half. During that same period the capital gains tax rate has been reduced 40% from 25% to 15%.

Eliminate the special tax rate on long term capital gains and treat them the same as other earnings. Income is income. This is nothing but a gift to the wealthiest 1% who hold the vast majority of investments that trigger capital gains. This is the biggest reason why the wealthiest are gaining an ever increasing piece of the wealth pie. Some are making billions and paying only 15% tax on it, not to mention not having to pay Social Security or Medicare taxes on this income. I would create some exception amount for people who sell their small business, as this is frequently their retirement plan and a one time event.

Some will argue the rate should be lower because the corporations already paid tax on this money so this would be double tax. Not really. I think we have enough examples of how many major corporations making billions in profits are paying little or no taxes. Let's consider how stock prices increase and generate capital gains. The average price to earnings ratio of the S&P 500 is about 20 times. That means that on average if a company is earning $1.00 per share their stock sells for $20 per share. So if a company's earnings increase by an additional dollar per share they may pay $.30 in additional taxes (only if they are paying in the highest of tax brackets which few are) for a net earnings per share increase of $.70. Based on this the stock goes up $14.00 ($.70 x 20). So the company pays an additional $.30 in taxes and the wealthy investor earns $14.00 and pays $2.10 in capital gains tax if they sell the shares. Does it look like anyone in this scenario paid too much tax on the earnings or gains?

So our friends in Congress, bent on protecting the wealthiest, will claim that they will not invest if the tax is increased and therefore the markets will decline hurting everyone's investments and 401K's. Not likely. If you had $100 and could invest it and earn $10.00 in capital gains but had to pay $4.00 in capital gains tax would you do it? Warren Buffet has stated that investors will invest if there is a profit to be made. I don't think we need him to tell us. If you can make a profit, you do it. Sure, there is a point where higher returns are demanded for riskier investments but the average person is not investing in junk bonds and startup companies. What else will these people do with their money? If they don't like the tax let them stuff their millions in their mattresses. See how much that earns.

b. The Middle - Everyone has to do their part. A 1% or so increase in tax rates for them. These people are essentially spending 100% of their net income so every dollar we take in taxes comes directly out of the economy. We all understand the masses drive the economy so this likely has to wait until the economy picks up, if it ever does.

c. The Poor – Cut the rewards for irresponsibility. You make your bed, lie in it. Limit the Earned Income Credit to only biological or legally adopted children. No nieces, step children or any of the others these people are faking. Limit the Child Tax Credit to a maximum of two children. Give these people free birth control instead. It would be a lot cheaper.

Limit both of these credits to U.S. Citizens. If you want the benefits of citizenship, become a Citizen. Also, if two unmarried people live in one house only one can claim the credits. No divvying up the kids or lying about being married to maximize the benefit.

We should even require proof that the children qualify. Make people present birth certificates or adoption papers the first time they claim a child. Put the onus on tax preparers to verify the information or subject them to stiff fines.

Corporate Income Taxes:

When it comes to corporate taxes this is a much more difficult issue. Large corporations, in particular, operate in many states and countries. Like it or not, we need to allow corporations to earn an attractive return on equity if they are going to continue in existence and continue to hire employees.

One difference with corporations is that they can be based wherever they want. We still have one of the highest corporate tax rates in the world, though taxes are lessened somewhat by the myriad of credits and special treatment of specific industries. If we over tax corporations, they can just pick up and "move" to some other country where taxes are lower. From a practical standpoint, it would be nearly impossible for General Electric to pack up and move to Switzerland. However, what they can do is create subsidiaries in those countries and do all of their non-U.S. business out of those locations and avoid U.S. taxes on profits in those foreign subsidiaries. In fact, they essentially have an obligation to their shareholders to do just that. Profits generated in these foreign subsidiaries are only taxable in the U.S. if they bring the cash onshore. Essentially they can delay this indefinitely.

Who cares if they move? Probably the tens of millions of Americans who work for big business.

So what should be done? We absolutely need to keep these companies doing as much of their production in goods or services from America.   Production includes both manufacturing tangible products as well as services. We must make our country as attractive as other countries. I believe we should reduce the top corporate tax rate by 10% to 15% for domestic profits. However, we should also eliminate many of the special provisions and credits that result in companies making billions in profits and paying little or no income taxes. A quick look at the profits and tax rates of some of America's largest corporations shows some astounding results.

Twelve Corporations: Their U.S. Pretax Profits and Their Federal Income Taxes, 2008–2010

$-millions

Company	2010 U.S. Profit	2009 U.S. Profit	2008 U.S. Profit	3 Year Total U.S. Profit	3 Year Total Fed Tax	3 Year Total Tax Rate
General Electric	5,079	(305)	2,948	7,722	(4,737)	-61.3%
American Electric Power	1,869	2,014	2,016	5,899	(545)	-9.2%
Dupont	949	180	995	2,124	(72)	-3.4%
Verizon Communications	11,963	12,261	8,294	32,518	(951)	-2.9%
Boeing	4,450	1,494	3,791	9,735	(178)	-1.8%
Wells Fargo	16,486	21,797	11,087	49,370	(681)	-1.4%
Honeywell International	1,243	1,723	1,937	4,903	(34)	-0.7%
IBM	8,861	9,404	8,208	26,473	1,001	3.8%
Yahoo	855	354	453	1,662	145	8.7%
United Technologies	2,543	2,539	2,854	7,936	792	10.0%
Exxon Mobil	7,419	2,490	9,745	19,654	2,782	14.2%
	61,717	53,951	52,328	167,996	(2,478)	-1.5%

Source: Citizens for Tax Justice

There it is. $167 billion in profits over three years and a negative tax paid. Sure some of this is because of investments in equipment and accelerated depreciation, some from carry forward of losses from prior years but wow. Something must change.

As noted earlier, the U.S. Tax Code is incredibly complex and making these changes would be complex and mired in politics. These big corporations make large contributions to candidates and their political parties. In addition, because of limits on contributions to candidates they throw their money around by funding projects in the home districts of our congressional representatives. This buys them great favor with our elected representatives. Only the voters can overcome this obstacle by voting out representatives who don't support the wishes of their electorate and by telling their representatives what they want. This is something the voting public often fails to do. In fact, most of the voting public doesn't even vote. If we don't change this nothing will change in our country and all decisions will be driven by who has the most money.

These are the same companies who claim they cannot be competitive in the U.S. because of the high corporate tax rates. Given a simplified tax structure with less credits and accelerated deductions they would be paying significantly more in taxes. However, the lower tax rate would benefit the smaller companies or those doing business only in the U.S. who can't move operations overseas in order to avoid taxes. Making these smaller and U.S. based companies more competitive would likely result in job growth in the U.S.

In addition, in order to encourage companies to repatriate foreign profits we should offer a significantly lower tax rate on foreign profits when the funds are brought back to the U.S. This could represent found money, so a rate of 5% to 10% could result in a multibillion dollar tax windfall for the U.S. Government as billions in offshore profits make their way back to the U.S.

Healthcare:

The countries with the highest ranked health care systems in the world have public health care. Why are people in the U.S. so adamantly opposed to this? Is it because they feel they are paying for health care for the freeloaders? Is it because they feel government will manage a failed system fraught with abuse and over charges? Is it because they already have great coverage and don't give a damn about people who do not have health insurance? Whatever the reasons, we can see from other countries that such a system can work well for all people.

The Centers for Disease Control and Prevention estimated that 22% of Americans (59 million) do not have health insurance. More than two out of five individuals who are uninsured at some point during the past year had one or more chronic diseases and this is based on just a partial list of chronic diseases. Approximately 15 million of the people without health insurance had high blood pressure, diabetes or asthma. People with such conditions often end up in emergency rooms and require treatment, paid for by hospitals or taxpayers, that is far more expensive than providing preventive care.

Our health care spending is off the chart when compared to almost any other country in the world. Despite the fact that over one in five Americans lack coverage and many don't have access to proper care, the U.S. still spends 83% more per capita on health care than the OECD average yet we still have a shorter life expectancy. That's probably because those with higher income, good jobs and health insurance live longer and those without die younger, bringing the average down. So who cares, the poor and uninsured deserve to die younger as punishments for not having better jobs or more money anyway, right?

Why is our health care so expensive? We already talked about the excessive tests run by doctors out of fear of lawsuits. Certainly another reason is that primary care physicians in the United States earn over $180,000 per year, compared with about half that amount in France and Australia. Orthopedic surgeons in the U.S earn on average over $440,000 per year, compared with $154,000 in France and $324,000 in the UK. Now these guys are some of our brightest and most educated people so I am not proposing they struggle to make ends meet - I want the best and smartest guy working on my spine when I am in a car accident. However, what if our orthopedic surgeons only made $300,000 per year? I think they could have a comfortable life. What if, in exchange, they didn't have to worry about mountains of paperwork or deal with the constant threat of lawsuits?

As the following chart shows, the cost of health care in America dwarfs that of any other developed nation.

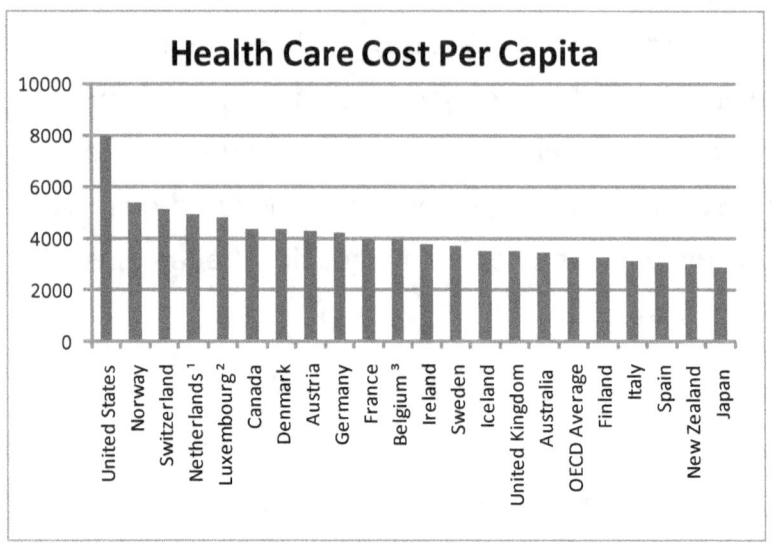

Source: OECD

In no uncertain terms, health care as we know it today in the U.S. is broken. The system simply does not work. When something is broken, we generally fix it. Not when it comes to health care in the U.S. Instead, we are mired in political infighting both in Congress and among the American people. When a corporation is in trouble and not performing, the Board of Directors fires management and brings in new leadership who restructure operations sometimes in very radical ways. The common term used in the business community is reengineering. It is definitely time for a radical shift in the American health care system.

When President Obama was working to pass the health care reform, many people were up in arms in opposition to any public option. Why are they so afraid of this possibility? This is how we provide health care for veterans. Certainly everyone fears a bloated, expensive government run system. I can't help but wonder if any of these people realize that the most productive and least expensive health care systems in the world are actually public systems. Certainly many that rank much higher than the U.S. system are.

What is it about us that makes us so afraid to change something we all know is totally broken? What can we do to it that we fear so much? Our members of Congress want to fix Medicare, or worse yet, foist it upon the private medical insurance industry. People often point to our broken and mismanaged Medicare system as evidence as to why we don't want a public health care system. They claim government can't manage it. Perhaps Medicare does need some changes, or perhaps it is simply inadequately funded. Could it be the Medicare tax is just too low? Why don't our congressional leaders ever raise that as the issue? The answer may not be to continually cut payments to health care providers. Maybe the answer is a new health care system.

The real problem is that we actually have the best health care in the world, if you happen to have great health care coverage or a lot of money. If you are part of the 150 million Americans classified as poor then it probably isn't so great for you. Health care systems that rank higher than ours do so because they provide better care for the entire population on average. America says too bad if you are poor. Got to some clinic or emergency room when it's too late and hope they can do something for you.

Why is it that a private health insurance company can pay their CEO $100 million (that's about 2,000 times the average household income in America) in a single year but they can't earn enough to deliver an adequate return to their shareholders without constantly raising rates by multiples of inflation, denying coverage to seemingly healthy people and denying claims for obscure technicalities?

Why is it that countries like France or Italy can effectively manage a public health care system yet we, in the greatest nation on earth, our words, cannot do the same? Are these nations that much smarter than us? How do they deliver better care for less money? I believe our concern is more with the incompetent boobs who run our country. A government that today has perhaps the lowest level of citizen approval of any time in our history. In spite of them, I think we must move forward with a new paradigm.

The problem with our government attempting to implement such a concept is that they think it is necessary to totally abandon the current system on a massive scale. Such a strategy requires that people with little real management experience conceive of every possible scenario and develop a one thousand page piece of legislation addressing every possibility, or so they think. Our legislators, in their quest for total control, believe they must direct the mindless drones in every aspect of a government run system. Think back to the education system in Finland where federal rules are simply guidelines to be followed by teaching professionals running their schools, resulting in limited regulation, competent management and the highest rated education system in the world.

In the real world of business, we would develop a framework, do focus groups to get potential user or customer feedback and then beta test the product in a real world environment.

I believe we should implement a system somewhat like the French system. Yes it would be government run, at least partially. If other countries can do it, we can too. Such a system would include coverage for everyone. Certainly attracting quality physicians would be the biggest hurdle, as we would require quality physicians who would be willing to work for a little less. Perhaps with a reduction in paperwork and elimination of exposure from lawsuits there would be an attraction for them. Management would be incented like those in private enterprise with incentives for cutting costs but only if they deliver quality service. With huge buying power such a system could negotiate competitive pricing with suppliers.

Most people think this cannot work because government screws up everything. They will inevitably point to Medicare. A large part of the problem with Medicare is simply that it is very inadequately funded. Annual outlays for Social Security and Medicare are almost equal yet the Social Security tax rate is over four times as high. Sure, there is fraud but this exists in private health care and insurance on a massive scale. Workers compensation and disability systems are riddled with fraud. Like any business enterprise, it's a matter of hiring competent management and holding them accountable. This system should be overseen by a board of directors made up of business leaders, physicians and academics with the power to set strategy and appoint management. Congress can have no management role or failure is imminent.

All people would be entitled to health care regardless of economic status. They would obtain their care, including preventative care, at public health care facilities. Those with more financial means could still patronize private facilities or pay extra for more specialized or superior facilities and health care providers. In public facilities, people would give up the right to sue for malpractice except in the most egregious cases of negligence. Quality of care would be overseen by doctors, not bureaucrats. Certainly doctors would not be free to be negligent and cause harm to patients and still continue to work at public facilities. Protection from lawsuits would not include protection of their jobs.

In order to test such a system we should implement it in a limited geographic area and evaluate the benefits and processes. After an adequate test period the service area would be expanded in increments as the process and administration is improved. Between 2002 and 2007, the cumulative growth in health insurance premiums was 78% compared with cumulative inflation of 17%. What do we have to lose? The 37th best health care system in the developed world that costs 83% more per capita than the average of other developed nations? This will never improve if we, as a nation, are not prepared to take some bold steps in a new direction.

Education:

Here again the U.S. stands alone. We spend 35% more per capita on education than the OECD average yet our students ranked 25th out of 40 countries in international testing. Of the thirty OECD member countries and some nonmember countries included in an OECD education cost analysis, only Luxembourg, Switzerland and Norway spent more per capita on secondary education than the U.S.

Proficiency in math and science skills will propel us to leadership status in the future. It is the scientists and engineers who develop and design new products and create technology breakthroughs. Clearly the U.S. graduates less engineering and science majors per capita than almost any country in the world. We do know one thing; we have the best higher education system in the world. That's why there are so many foreign students at our top universities. Many of the engineers we graduate are not American. However our own schools are not preparing enough students to succeed in these majors in college. 59% of all doctoral degrees and 43% of all higher-education degrees in engineering and science in the U.S. are awarded to temporary residents. Does this sound like a country that will continue to be a world leader in the decades to come? Technology companies are lobbying for more work visas so they can bring more foreign workers to the

U.S. to fill these jobs.

The problem with our schools is twofold: First, they are frequently run by politicians, many with no real education background who develop rigid standards and second, we fail to see the value in good teachers and do not adequately reward them in terms of compensation. Teachers, or potential teachers with advanced knowledge in math and science, are more in demand in the outside world and can make more money there. Why don't our schools pay more to attract these people? Regardless of the subject matter, we need the best teaching our leaders and innovators of tomorrow.

Of course this is not only the fault of our schools. We are a nation built on greed. We all want to earn as much money as possible.   I have to have more than the Jones's. It's a competition where the person with the biggest house and nicest car wins. In Finland it's an honor to be a teacher, and the best and brightest with advanced degrees go into the teaching profession.

Let's look at it this way. If a person with a passion for science gets an advanced education they may go out into the world and make a difference. Maybe help discover a new life saving drug. If instead that person becomes a teacher and shows that passion to students, they may, over their career, inspire one hundred students to work hard and enter the field of science. Now that one person's effort may have created one hundred people who may change the world. And if two of them become teachers and each inspire one hundred others... The benefit increases geometrically generation after generation.

Like health care, we have a broken system but are afraid to change it. Why? It can't get much worse. It is time for America to reinvent its education system. It isn't about money or spending cuts. Charter schools and catholic schools over achieve while spending less per student.

I am neither an educator nor an expert on education. So I can't profess to tell anyone how to fix such a complex issue. But I do understand that when something has proven not to work for years and continues to deteriorate we need to consider alternatives, sometimes radical change. We are failing our youth and doing nothing about it. We must study some of the more successful education systems in the world and model our system after the best aspects of each of them. Like health care, there is no reason to assume we have to implode the entire system in one fell swoop. In fact we can't because education is managed at the local level. The federal government does not manage our schools.

What the Federal Government can do is issue guidelines and withhold funds from those who don't comply. Many of America's school districts are in dire financial condition. The Federal Government should select several school districts and provide additional federal funding if they agree to a new model, one managed by educators, one willing to do what it takes to attract the right teachers. These micro school districts can be manageable and a test case for a more national school model.

Our system fails to attract the people we need because we refuse to reward the type of teachers we need most. What could we lose if we establish a test school district and reinvent how we educate students in America? Can we get any worse than twenty fifth out of forty? The closest we have come to changing our failing system is establishing a few charter schools which are available for only a small percentage of students.

In our test district, management would be by a board consisting of educators with no direct political ties. Government intervention would consist solely of general requirements. Teachers would be compensated based on demand and their level of education. There are certainly many quality teachers in frustrating situations who would relish an opportunity to implement a game changing system. Not everyone works only with the interest of making the most possible money in their lives. Of course, such an effort would take a number of years before we could determine if it is effective. But, if we don't start somewhere we will just continue to languish at the bottom. Is that good enough for the United States of America? Every empire in the history of the world has collapsed eventually. Our time may be sooner than we think. While we won't simply collapse as a nation, we will certainly fall from our perch as the world's greatest nation that will continue to deteriorate over time. But don't worry; the top 1% will always live well.

Every politician talks about change when they campaign but none are really committed to it. Once elected none of them is really willing to implement wholesale change. No one wants to be the elected official who tried something new and failed. Instead they all fail because they fail to try. In business, we accept that sometimes we will fail. Innovation often grows out of failure. Most successful people have failed one or more times. We should reward those who are willing to take a chance to make something better. It's time for our leadership to stop worrying only about reelection and start worrying about moving America forward or step aside.

Big Business:

So many of our largest corporate citizens pay little or no, or even negative taxes on billions of dollars in profits. As mentioned in the section of this chapter on Corporate Income Taxes, we do need to lower the tax rate on corporations. However, we also need to eliminate the special provisions that help big business pay no taxes. It's pretty hard to imagine that General Electric can't be competitive if their tax rate is over seven percent. If that's the case, I would have to assume management is not competent and needs to be replaced.

It seems obvious that change is needed. Why don't we fix the tax code? Two reasons:

1. These big companies are owned by the wealthiest Americans who also happen to be the big contributors to election campaign funds. Think back to the discussion of who is contributing to Mitt Romney's SuperPAC. $1 million from one executive and his wife at Romney's former company Bain Capital. They invest in corporations. Does anyone think they want these companies to pay more taxes? So what do you suppose $1 million dollars buys in terms of how Romney will vote on matters of importance to these corporations or their shareholders? Romney's Super PAC is receiving millions of dollars from large venture

capital firms. It is simply an effort to ensure the perpetuation of the tremendous tax benefits these companies and their wealthy investors enjoy. With Romney in office, the wealth and income gap in America will continue to grow.

2. The big companies themselves are contributing to campaigns or pouring money into programs in congressional districts where they want to buy a congressman. So a big company spends $10 million on a social initiative in a particular congressman's district and then gains support for a legislative change that will save them many multiples of what they contributed. Think back to the earlier example when Congress threatened to let a loophole beneficial to General Electric expire in 2008. Representative Charles Rangel was then chairman of the Ways and Means Committee, which would decide the fate of the tax break. Mr. Rangel soon reversed his opposition to the tax break. The following month GE announced that its foundation had donated $11 million to benefit various schools in Mr. Rangel's district. Did GE buy a congressman's vote? Was this a bribe? Certainly by my definition of a bribe it seems so.

Of course, we could never stop this behavior. What school district is going to say no to millions of dollars? What congressman is going to refuse funds that will greatly benefit their constituents? The circle is again complete. GE got their tax break, representative Rangel got some happy voters and the voters got their library. In the end didn't everyone benefit? Not exactly. Ultimately all of us taxpayers somehow have to make up for GE's tax savings.

Of course, these politicians will tell you we need these low taxes to promote job growth. Companies will hire when there is demand for their product and more profit can be made, not when taxes are lower. Consider the following chart of maximum tax rates versus unemployment.

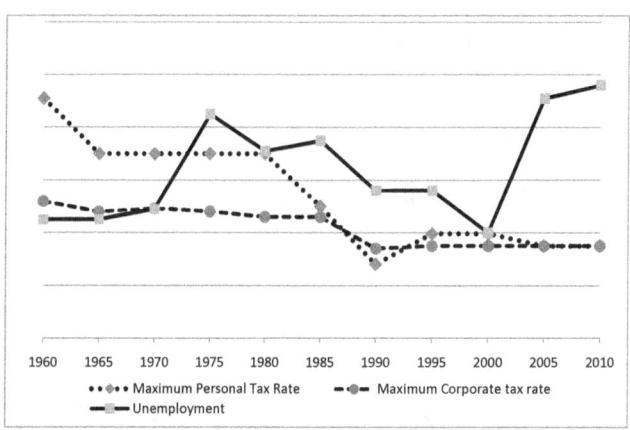

As the chart shows in the 1960's and 1970's, while tax rates were declining, unemployment was rising. In the 1980's and 1990's tax rates and unemployment both declined. Beginning in 2000 the unemployment rate rose sharply in spite of level or slightly declining tax rates. American voters can no longer allow those legislators wishing to protect the few to mislead them about the relationship between taxes and unemployment. It is simply a ploy to reduce taxes on the wealthy.

Unfortunately, it's too late to go back and undo some of the excessive bailouts of banks and investment banks. Not that we should have let them go under, but perhaps they should have absorbed more of the loss. Who owns the stock in these companies? Correct, the top 1%. Now I think we see why Goldman had to get 100% payback on their credit default swaps. After all, how else could their CEO take home $40 million? It's no accident that the Secretary of the Treasury when Goldman was totally bailed out was a former Goldman CEO.

Another action that could help to preserve jobs in America is to force countries like China to "play fair." Few would disagree that they do not. Our private enterprises must compete with their government subsidized companies and currency. Absent a level playing field, we should tax products coming from China. We cannot continue to send hundreds of billions of dollars to China every year. Their economy is growing; more of their people are prospering, while less and less of our citizens are prospering. Why don't we do something about this? Let me pose this question: who owns the companies that are making their goods in China and therefore prospering greatly from the low cost when they sell their gods in America or elsewhere? I doubt I have to answer that for you. What an intelligence audience.

Our friends in Washington, who won't take action on this, will tell you we need free trade. They will tell you that if we tax these products China will stop importing our goods and that will kill American jobs. That is actually true. Let's take that a step further. The net outflow to China is somewhere around $350 billion per year. So who needs who more?

Our lawmakers will likely tell you we can increase jobs in America by our companies and their workers being more competitive. How would we do that? Let's see, we could lower corporate taxes. Wait, these big multi nationals are not paying enough in taxes to have lowering them make a difference. Ah yes, I have solved the riddle. We need to reduce the minimum wage to $1.50 per hour. No benefits. No job safety regulations. No pollution restrictions. Done. We can now compete head to head. I just solved the unemployment problem. I should be President.

Aside from all of these actions that our Congress will never take, there is one thing we, the people of America can do. We can stop supporting this outsourcing of our jobs to other countries. We, as a group, can force change without legislation. Buy American. You hear it every day but no one really pays attention. We all think, what is one shirt or one new toaster going to matter. The answer is not at all, but one million toasters will matter, a lot. Amazingly almost every item sold in the gift shops in the Smithsonian and many of the monuments in Washington D.C. are made in China or other countries. ABC News reported that if we all spent $3.33 on an American made product we would create 10,000 new jobs. I'm not going to check their math but I believe it.

How can we get Congress to pass legislation on corporate taxes and doing business with China? We simply need so many private citizens to tell them by phone, mail or email what we want. The hard part is organizing such a grass roots effort. The wealthy who contribute $500,000 get heard. They know what they want. Even though they are outnumbered ninety seven to three, their voice is louder. The average person can't call their Congressman and tell him or her, "I want you to eliminate the accelerated depreciation provisions on solar energy turbine equipment and corporate jets and stop allowing public companies to deduct the value of stock options granted to executives based on the value at exercise." How could they? Few people have a clue what these things mean. Does that mean we should ignore what is best for them? No, we simply need leaders in our government who care about the 97%. Our current congressional members either don't care or simply don't understand. In either case we need new leadership.

Regardless of economic and social position, we all still get only one vote. The single mother on welfare gets the same vote as Bill Gates and Warren Buffet. The problem is, that mother probably doesn't understand the issues and likely doesn't get out and vote. But organizing disenchanted voters who are barely surviving and trying to educate them on such matters is a more monumental task than just letting Americans suffer and watching our country decline. Hopefully this book contributes toward educating them on basic financial and governmental issues in a short, readily understandable format.

Epilogue

"We hold these truths to be self-evident, that all men are created equal, that they are endowed by their Creator with certain unalienable Rights, that among these are Life, Liberty and the pursuit of Happiness. — That to secure these rights, Governments are instituted among Men, deriving their just powers from the consent of the governed, — <u>That whenever any Form of Government becomes destructive of these ends, it is the Right of the People to alter or to abolish it, and to institute new Government, laying its foundation on such principles and organizing its powers in such form, as to them shall seem most likely to effect their Safety and Happiness.</u>"

U.S. Declaration of Independence

APPENDIX

U.S. Policy Budget Authority and Outlays by Function
(in millions of dollars)

	2011	2012
050 National Defense:		
Department of Defense-Military:		
Military personnel	151,826	154,057
Operation and maintenance	294,122	294,891
Procurement	134,165	128,051
Research, development, test and evaluation	80,905	75,722
Other	72,299	43,244
Payments to the Military Retirement Fund	4,950	5,475
Other	(495)	(266)
Atomic energy defense activities:	1,545	1,732
Total, National defense	**739,317**	**702,906**
150 International affairs:		
International development and humanitarian assistance:	33,031	26,274
International security assistance:	8,279	15,965
State Department operations	8,740	12,018
Embassy security, construction, and maintenance	1,724	1,801
Contributions to international organizations	1,683	1,619
Assessed contributions for international peacekeeping	2,125	1,920
Other conduct of foreign affairs	20,007	25,667
Total, International affairs	**75,589**	**85,264**

250 General science, space, and technology:

General science and basic research:	13,260	14,293
Space flight, research, and supporting activities:	17,748	18,155
Total, General science, space, and technology	**31,008**	**32,448**

270 Energy:

Energy supply:	4,129	4,189
Energy conservation:	1,104	2,063
Energy preparedness	255	(447)
Energy information, policy, and regulation:	458	398
Naval petroleum reserves oil and gas sales	(1,286)	(1,210)
Tennessee Valley Authority	1,048	1,125
Recovery Act grants in lieu of energy tax credits	4,754	6,481
Energy conservation:	5,347	147
Total, Energy	**15,809**	**12,746**

300 Natural resources and environment:

Water resources:	7,978	8,115
Conservation and land management:	10,099	9,308
Recreational resources:	3,683	3,844
Pollution control and abatement:	9,747	9,052
National Oceanic and Atmospheric Administration	4,816	5,567
United States Geological Service and other	1,435	1,596
Total, Natural resources and environment	**37,758**	**37,482**

350 Agriculture:

Farm income stabilization:	1,790	1,962
Research and education programs	2,047	1,626
Animal and plant inspection programs	913	948
Other	1,648	1,622
Commodity Credit Corporation	7,881	5,316
Crop insurance	6,994	3,142
Other	2,454	1,320
Agricultural research and services:	437	390
Total, Agriculture	**24,164**	**16,326**

370 Commerce and housing credit:
Mortgage credit:

Federal Housing Administration loan programs	2,177	302
Government National Mortgage Association	(696)	(598)
Other mortgage credit	4,930	464
Small and minority business assistance	822	849
Economic and demographic statistics	1,320	1,138
Other	(937)	(897)
Troubled Asset Relief Program	(43,168)	-0--
Total, Commerce and housing credit	**(35,552)**	**1,258**

400 Transportation:

Ground transportation:	1,156	(107)
Air transportation:	18,907	18,558
Water transportation:	8,757	8,698
Highways	43,359	72,040
Mass transit	10,633	22,337
Other	9,738	22,273
Total, Transportation	**92,550**	**143,799**

450 Community and regional development:

Other community development programs	6,206	5,149
Rural development	862	712
Indian programs	2,320	2,009
Other	223	55
Disaster relief	7,565	6,924
Total, Community and regional development	**17,176**	**14,849**

500 Education, training, employment, and social services:
Elementary, secondary, and vocational education:

Education for the disadvantaged	15,914	15,412
Impact aid	1,276	1,276
School improvement	5,303	3,412
English language acquisition	750	750
Special education	12,587	12,020
Vocational and adult education	2,016	1,683

Indian education	927	921
Innovation and improvement	1,389	4,995
Other	3,896	1,806
Total, Elementary, secondary, and vocational education	44,058	42,275
Higher education:		
Student financial assistance	43,682	42,944
Federal family education loan program	(24,493)	(2,110)
Federal direct loan program	(22,087)	(22,710)
American Opportunity Tax Credit	3,861	4,416
Other higher education programs	4,145	3,602
Total, Higher education	5,108	26,142
Research and general education aids:	3,848	3,852
Training and employment:	7,553	6,684
Labor law, statistics, and other administration	2,051	1,987
Children and families services programs	9,315	9,795
Other	5,003	4,894
Total, Social services	27,770	27,212
Research and general education aids:	1,384	1,376
Social services:		
Social services block grant	1,785	1,785
Rehabilitation services - Department of Education	3,085	3,122
Other social services	535	535
Total, Social services	5,405	5,442
Total, Education, training, employment, and social services	**83,725**	**102,447**

550 Health:

Health care services	22,087	21,298
National Institutes of Health	30,786	31,829
Other health research and training	2,518	600
Food safety and inspection	1,019	1,011
Occupational and mine safety and health	938	1,002
Food and Drug Administration	2,362	2,744
Consumer Product Safety Commission	118	122
Grants to States for Medicaid	260,783	270,428
Other	56,889	39,867
Total, Health	**377,500**	**368,901**

570 Medicare:

Medicare Administrative expenses	5,934	7,324
Hospital insurance	259,947	262,093
Supplementary medical insurance	231,179	237,624
Medicare prescription drug	66,082	62,080
Premiums and collections	(68,359)	(76,450)
Total, Medicare	**494,783**	**492,671**

600 Income security:

Unemployment insurance program administrative	3,633	3,309
Housing assistance	43,348	43,659
Food and nutrition assistance:	8,058	7,865
Refugee assistance	731	825
Low income home energy assistance	5,100	2,570
Child care and development block grant	2,127	2,927
Supplemental security income Administrative	3,545	3,875

Federal civilian employee retirement and disability	73,287	75,894
Military retirement	55,475	48,455
Unemployment insurance (UI) programs	132,280	92,707
Food and nutrition assistance	98,260	105,290
Supplemental security income (SSI)	52,454	47,788
Child support and family support programs	4,065	3,505
Temporary assistance for needy families	17,393	17,671
Child care entitlement to states	2,917	2,917
Foster care and adoption assistance	6,622	7,006
Earned income tax credit (EITC)	44,940	46,495
Child tax credit	22,924	25,136
Making Work Pay Tax Credit	13,876	-0--
Other	13,689	7,697
Total, Income security	**604,724**	**545,591**

650 Social security:

Old-age and survivors insurance administrative expenses	2,973	3,213
Disability insurance administrative expenses	2,824	3,124
Old-age and survivors insurance	600,680	627,844
Disability insurance	129,152	135,696
Other	14,661	318
Total, Social security	**750,290**	**770,195**

700 Veterans benefits and services:

Hospital and medical care for veterans	50,476	52,585
Veterans housing	1,294	359
National Cemetery Administration	296	297
Departmental administration	5,962	5,737

Other	1,424	1,303
Compensation and pensions	53,978	58,090
Veterans education, training, and rehabilitation	10,261	10,941
Total, Veterans benefits and services	**123,691**	**129,312**

750 Administration of justice:

Federal law enforcement activities:		
Criminal investigations (DEA, FBI, DHS, FinCEN, ICDE)	5,896	5,372
Alcohol, tobacco, firearms, and explosives investigations	1,120	1,147
Border and transportation security directorate activities	22,711	22,668
Other law enforcement activities	3,930	4,057
Federal litigative and judicial activities	10,837	11,194
Federal prison system and detention trustee program	7,627	8,386
High-intensity drug trafficking areas program	239	200
State and Local Law Enforcement Assistance	1,697	1,141
Crime victims fund, discretionary change	(5,820)	(6,641)
Adjustment for 2011 CR versus 2011 Request	2,436	-0--
Other justice programs	1,909	1,877
Immigration and customs fees	(5,327)	(5,272)
Treasury forfeiture fund	1,017	1,214
Other mandatory law enforcement programs	237	242
Federal litigative and judicial activities:	2,612	2,629
Criminal justice assistance	6,536	8,133
Total, Administration of justice	**57,657**	**56,347**

800 General government:

Legislative functions:		
Tax administration	11,507	12,606
Treasury claims and judgments	4,528	2,692
Legislative branch discretionary programs	4,026	4,251
Build American Bond Payments, Recovery Act	2,814	3,589
Other general purpose fiscal assistance	2,608	2,664
Other fiscal operations	1,484	995
Total, General property and records management	1,091	1,069
Other	2,123	1,658
Total, General government	**30,181**	**29,524**

900 Net interest:

Interest on Treasury debt securities (gross):	430,414	474,146
Interest received by on-budget trust funds:	(64,341)	(66,863)
Interest received by social security trust funds	(115,739)	(113,340)
Other interest:	(43,646)	(52,345)
Total, Net interest	**206,688**	**241,598**

920 Allowances:

Allowance for Future Disaster Costs	10,000	10,000
Adjustment for 2011 CR versus 2011 Request	712	-0--
Total, Allowances	**10,712**	**10,000**

950 Undistributed offsetting receipts:

Employing agency contributions, military retirement	(25,965)	(27,503)
Employing agency contributions, DOD Retiree Health	(11,316)	(11,150)
Employing agency contributions, Civil Service Retirement	(18,739)	(19,161)
Postal Service contributions, Civil Service Retirement and Disability	(3,707)	(3,800)
Contributions to HI trust fund	(4,033)	(3,987)

Contributions to employee retirement and disability	(3,317)	(3,451)
Employer Contributions to social security	(15,138)	(15,205)
Rents and royalties on the Outer Continental Shelf	(5,223)	(7,343)
Proceeds from Sale of Securities from AIG		
Credit Facility Trust	(2,017)	(4,035)
Other undistributed offsetting receipts:	(200)	(4,000)
Total, Undistributed offsetting receipts	**(89,655)**	**(99,635)**
Total Federal Budget ($3.6 trillion)	**3,648,115**	**3,694,029**

Note: Many line items were combined in the above table. The detailed budget available on the White House web site contains over two thousand lines of data.

www.ingramcontent.com/pod-product-compliance
Lightning Source LLC
Chambersburg PA
CBHW070003300526
45794CB00001B/172